D1500303

Originally published by Christian Art Publishers
under the title *A Shelter from the Storm*

This edition © 2010 Christian Art Gifts, RSA
                            Christian Art Gifts Inc., IL, USA

Second edition 2017

Devotions written by Solly Qzrovech

Images used under license from Shutterstock.com

Designed by Christian Art Gifts

Scripture quotations are taken from the *Holy Bible*, New International
Version® NIV®. Copyright © 1973, 1978, 1984 by International Bible
Society. Used by permission of Zondervan Publishing House. All rights
reserved.

Printed in China

ISBN 978-1-4321-2498- 4

18 19 20 21 22 23 24 25 26 27 – 11 10 9 8 7 6 5 4 3 2

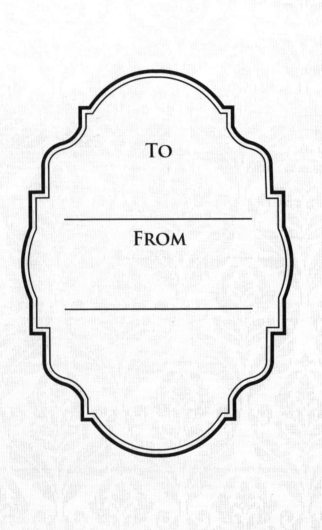

To

_____

From

_____

A
SHELTER
FROM THE
STORM

CHRISTIAN ART
PUBLISHERS

JANUARY

HOPE AND RENEWAL

A NEW HOPE

Trust in the LORD with all your heart and lean not on your own understanding; in all your ways acknowledge Him, and He will make your paths straight. (Proverbs 3:5-6)

Today is the first day of the new year – and of the rest of your life. Decisions you make today could have far-reaching consequences in your life. Spend some time constructively in God's presence today. Begin by confessing the sins and weaknesses that have hindered you in the past, and experience God's wonderful forgiveness. Then you will start the new year with a clean slate.

This will lay a solid foundation for your life this year, a life built on trust in the living Christ. He will never disappoint you. Through the Holy Spirit, He will open up new horizons of what life can offer you. Your values will change as you start looking at life through His eyes. The more closely you walk with Him, the more clearly you will understand all that He can do in and through your life.

At the beginning of this new year, resolve to strengthen and enrich your relationship with Christ so that you can blossom and be as fruitful as He desires you to be.

STARTING OVER

Therefore, if anyone is in Christ, he is a new creation; the old has gone, the new has come! (2 Corinthians 5:17)

New beginnings are exciting, even though there might be a possibility of failure. Do not allow such thoughts to prevent you from moving forward with hope and courage. Grab hold of every opportunity that presents itself this year, and trust that you will complete what you start in faith.

There is untold satisfaction in moving into the unknown with a deep sense of trust that your love for God and your unwavering faith in Him will make all things work together for your good. Positive spiritual thinking brings about positive spiritual results.

Enter the new year with an awareness of the presence of God in your life, knowing that He holds your destiny in His hands. Expect from His loving hand only what is best for you. Work and pray faithfully, knowing that His love is at work in your life every day. And should doubt bring discouragement and despair to you along the way, lay all this in prayer before the Father, and He will renew the hope in your soul.

A NEW BEGINNING DAWNS

He who was seated on the throne said,
"I am making everything new!" (Revelation 21:5)

Today is a new day, a new opportunity, presented to you by God. Yesterday, with all its disappointments and despair, belongs to the past. Do not look back; what is passed is passed. God is giving you a hope and a future.

God, in His infinite grace, is granting you the opportunity to rectify those things that have gone wrong in your life. Learn from your failures and mistakes, from your weaknesses and defeats. You have a precious opportunity to start anew. Assured of Christ's forgiving love, you can learn from your past experiences and decide, from now on, to live in obedience to the Master's commands and walk in His ways.

Turn to Christ and confess your weaknesses and shortcomings to Him. Open your heart for His Spirit to enter and take control of your life. Then face the future with confidence in the joyous knowledge that God is with you. If we allow Christ to make us new, we will handle life with maturity and we will experience the peace of God that transcends all understanding.

OUR UNCHANGING GOD!

I will instruct you and teach you in the way you should go; I will counsel you and watch over you. (Psalm 32:8)

The prospect of a new year could be exciting because of new possibilities and opportunities, but disquieting if you face the future with anxiety; wondering whether the problems and disasters of the past will repeat themselves. International crises, financial setbacks, as well as personal problems and disappointments, tend to cloud our vision of the future.

Remember, you can place your hope in the omniscience of God. He truly cares about you and He loves you deeply, "But because of His great love for us, God, who is rich in mercy, made us alive with Christ" (Eph. 2:4). But personal and social factors cause us to doubt and despair. Therefore, you will have to rediscover that in this loveless world there is still Somebody who has a special interest in you: a God in heaven who is Love and who loves you tenderly.

Believe in the promises of Jesus and approach the new year in His loving presence. He will guide you through the labyrinth of life because He knows what is best for you.

A NEW BEGINNING

One thing I do: Forgetting what is behind and straining toward what is ahead. (Philippians 3:13)

It is a sign of God's immeasurable grace that no person ever reaches a stage in life where he cannot start afresh. Every day that dawns is a new beginning. Our God is the God of the second chance.

But past failures might seem to have trapped you in a rut where hope and expectation have altogether died. Do not, however, allow whatever may have happened in the past to cause you to lose sight of what the future may hold.

If you wish to make a fresh start make a firm decision to be done with your old life, even though it will still try to influence your new way of living. It is also important to remember that all new life comes from God alone, who is the Source and Creator of all life. It is only as you acknowledge this that you will experience the regenerating power of the Holy Spirit. Continually affirm that new life flows through you as a result of God's grace, and you will receive the inheritance of new life that is yours in Christ.

THE POWER AND THE GLORY!

The LORD has established His throne in heaven, and His kingdom rules over all. (Psalm 103:19)

In a world where evil holds sway over truth and justice, we must never forget that the power and the sovereignty and the majesty reside in God. It is this knowledge that encourages and strengthens us even in our darkest hour.

History records many instances where it appeared as if all was lost: when anarchy and lawlessness threatened to destroy all goodness; when selfishness and lust dominated; when innocent people were oppressed and tortured.

But history also shows those times when truth and justice eventually triumphed. There may have been a time of anxiety and concern when fear and suffering were rife, but ultimately the power of evil was destroyed and the righteous prevailed.

However cheerless and hopeless circumstances may seem, never forget that God is almighty and great and that He is still in control. Place your trust in Jesus Christ your Redeemer and find encouragement and peace in the knowledge that our setbacks are merely temporary, because Christ has already conquered the world (see John 16:33).

TRUST IN GOD

"My grace is sufficient for you, for My power is made perfect in weakness." (2 Corinthians 12:9)

There are very few people who have never despaired at the inadequacy of their own resourcefulness, and who consequently feel that they simply cannot go on. These feelings may be the result of illness, death, loneliness, financial insecurity, or any of the numerous setbacks that can have a destructive influence on the human spirit and emotions.

In many cases, people regard their situation as hopeless, and then they run the risk of becoming completely discouraged. Whatever the predicament in which you find yourself, and however dark the prospect may seem, never underestimate the extent of God's love for you and the vastness of His grace.

Take a moment to consider the innumerable instances in the Bible and in the history of the world when God transformed despair into hope, and defeat into victory through His grace. However desperate your circumstances may seem to you, always remember that God loves you with an eternal love, and that He is waiting for you to turn to Him and trust in Him. Your faith will be rewarded, and in His own wonderful way He will deliver you.

A HOPE-FILLED HEART

Brothers, we do not want you to ... grieve like the rest of men, who have no hope. (1 Thessalonians 4:13)

Love ... always hopes. (1 Corinthians 13:6-7)

Hope and despair are found in the hearts of people, not in circumstances. And love causes hope to triumph. When things are at their darkest, love brings hope to light up the darkness of night. God has enough love to avert all despair. He has woven hope into our hearts so that we can trust in the future.

Martin Luther said that everything in the world is done in hope. The farmer would not sow seed if he did not hope for a harvest. A man would not marry if he did not hope for a happy family life. A business-man would not work hard if he did not hope for a good profit.

What oxygen does for the lungs, hope does for the soul: without it, we would die inwardly. When all is hopeless, then hope keeps us going. Hope is the battle of the soul that enables us to grasp eternity and the love of God. If it were not for hope, our hearts would be completely broken. Praise the Lord, for His love is infinite. He gives us hope through love.

HOPE FOR THE FUTURE

"Has He not made with me an everlasting covenant, arranged and secured in every part?" (2 Samuel 23:5)

Many people are overburdened with worry and their future seems dark and unsure. Deep anxiety is caused by carrying the heavy burden of daily responsibilities. Unless you have a strong faith, this could have far-reaching effects on your physical, emotional, and mental well-being.

The Son of the Most High God died and rose from the dead to set you free from this burden of worry. God loved you so much that Jesus Christ gave His life to redeem you from the terrible burden of anxious worries. Through His death and resurrection, Christ gives the glorious assurance to all who believe in Him, and who accept Him as Savior and Redeemer, that they will receive the reward of eternal life when they will be with Him forever.

There is no doubt about this promise. You have the Word of the living God Himself as guarantee. Unlike those who have no hope, you are blessed with the assurance that the Savior died in order that you may live. Regardless of the circumstances that you may find yourself in, this assurance should be a great comfort and encouragement.

LIVING HOPE AND TRUE FAITH!

Praise be to the God and Father of our Lord Jesus Christ! In His great mercy He has given us new birth into a living hope through the resurrection of Jesus Christ from the dead. (1 Peter 1:3)

Let your anxious heart rejoice with the glorious expectations of all the riches and treasures that await you in heaven. Thank God for that and let this prayer help you to turn your thoughts away from all the burdens and worries of this world. Renew your mind with thoughts of the pure, unspoilt inheritance that is waiting for you – an inheritance that cannot be destroyed. That's worth praising about!

Prayer focuses our hearts on heaven, even while our feet are firmly planted on the earth. Peter prays here for Christians who are facing brutal persecutions as well as the rejection of family and friends. Through this prayer he reminds them of the inheritance that is waiting for them in heaven, even though they are involved in such a bitter struggle here on earth.

Make sure that you have laid up treasures in heaven – otherwise your life, seen from the perspective of eternity, is worthless.

BETWEEN HOPE AND DESPAIR

What a wretched man I am! Who will rescue me from this body of death? (Romans 7:24)

Christ never promised that those who follow Him would always remain on the mountaintop. On the contrary, He Himself sent His disciples into the valley where they became intensely aware of their powerlessness and incompetence.

It is encouraging to know that even Paul experienced the depths of spiritual depression, yet he rose to great heights where he was able to praise God for victory. Although you will, at times, experience both hope and despair, you need to decide where you will habitually choose to live. God wants you to taste the joy and feel the strength that flow from your awareness of His loving presence in your life.

Too few of His children see themselves as victorious conquerors. They are so aware of their sinfulness, failures, and defeats that they cower behind their spiritual unworthiness instead of focusing on the abundant life that can be theirs through the power of the Holy Spirit in them. When you yield to His presence you will begin to live to His glory and become a worthy channel of His love and power.

A SPIRIT OF HOPE

Why are you downcast, O my soul? Why so disturbed within me? Put your hope in God, for I will yet praise Him, my Savior and my God. (Psalm 42:5)

It is very difficult to remain hopeful when you are depressed and everything you do seems doomed to fail. You can however fight this situation.

- ⚓ Believe that God is greater than your circumstances and any problems that are weighing you down. Accept the victory in His holy name. Remember, "In all things we are more than conquerors" (Rom. 8:37).
- ⚓ Lay your problems before the Father in earnest and specific prayer. Pour out all your problems before Him. You will be amazed at the results.
- ⚓ Believe steadfastly that God can and will achieve something glorious through this dark period in your life. "And we know that in all things God works for the good of those who love Him" (Rom. 8:28).
- ⚓ Make a conscious effort to turn your eyes away from yourself to see the world in need. God has a purpose in all things.

God is still on the throne and He is still in control.

GET OUT OF DISCOURAGEMENT

Though he stumble, he will not fall, for the LORD upholds him with His hand. (Psalm 37:24)

Most people know how it feels to be discouraged. It usually occurs when a long-cherished dream fails, or when noble plans collapse like a house of cards. If discouragement takes hold of your heart, your life becomes bitter and you may find it difficult to recover your vision.

If you are discouraged because of a dream or plan that failed, analyze the idea in relation to your discouragement. If you are convinced that the idea is worthwhile, reject the discouragement as the nonsense it really is. Keep the vision clearly in your mind, and do not allow it to be defeated by thoughts of failure.

It is also important to retain an inner strength that enables you to control your thoughts. When your spirit is sound and healthy, it will limit negative thoughts. That is why it is important to cultivate a positive spirit.

The teachings of Jesus and the guidance of the Holy Spirit form the bulwark that helps you resist discouragement. Then you can achieve the goal that burns brightly in your heart.

IT IS WELL WITH MY SOUL

Why have You rejected us forever, O God? Why does Your anger smolder against the sheep of Your pasture? (Psalm 74:1)

There are many people who feel abandoned and completely forsaken. Their lives fall apart, and their only thought is, "Why?". They seem to live good lives, keeping God's commandments, and yet in their times of trial God seems to have forsaken them.

It is an absolutely false notion to think that you are abandoned or forsaken by God. He has promised to be with you always and never to forsake you (Heb. 13:5). He proved the unfathomable depth of His love by sacrificing His Son on the cross for you.

God has a divine purpose with everything that happens in your life. Even when you are the victim of adversity, don't despair. He wants to use these circumstances to bring about His perfect will in your life.

There was a brief moment on the cross when Jesus was abandoned by God, but the agony of Good Friday was transformed into the triumphant victory of Easter Sunday. Be assured, under all circumstances the living Christ is with you. Place your trust in Him, and in His time, you will experience victory.

DISCOURAGED?

Say to those with fearful hearts, "Be strong,
do not fear; your God will come." (Isaiah 35:4)

Discouragement manifests itself in different ways, but always leaves you disillusioned, wondering whether all your efforts are worth the trouble. If you feel that your dreams have been shattered and your efforts have come to nothing, do not allow self-pity to sow the seed of discouragement in your heart. You might be tempted to trust in sources of inspiration and strength of your own making. When these sources fail you, you lose your vision and life becomes empty and meaningless.

God is your only constant source of inspiration. He asks you to come and draw freely from Him. Then you will be able to overcome discouragement. Remember: God is waiting to work in partnership with you. He does not work against you, but seeks your cooperation at all times in order to neutralize the forces that depress and threaten to overcome you.

You do not battle against discouragement and depression alone. God is on your side and He is waiting to lift you up so that you can walk forward with joy and achieve the victory.

FIND ENCOURAGEMENT IN GOD

Open my eyes that I may see wonderful
things in Your law. (Psalm 119:18)

Despondency and discouragement are common in the world today. People's emotions rise and fall like mercury, creating an unstable and insecure existence. The result is that many people are unhappy and not very sure of themselves. This influences their actions, plans, and decisions negatively.

If you want to *live* as opposed to merely *existing*, it is important to stay positive. If things are going well now, enjoy life and thank God for the good things. If things are not going well, then you should analyze the situation, identify the problem, and deal with it.

You will need a faith that is strong enough to enable you to bear the afflictions, handle the problems, overcome the obstacles, and eventually live triumphantly. Such a faith is developed through prayer, through which you seek the assistance of the living Christ. Search the Scripture for examples of God's wondrous deeds. You will find one example after another where ordinary people were able to overcome difficulties in the strength of the Lord. Find your encouragement in Jesus Christ and in His Word and you will triumph over depression.

LIGHT IN THE DARKNESS

*To those who have been called, who are loved by God the
Father and kept by Jesus Christ: Mercy, peace and
love be yours in abundance. (Jude 1:1-2)*

The world seems to be in a perpetual state of chaos.
Apart from dozens of localized confrontations between nations and factions, there have been two world
wars in the past century. Lawlessness and violence
are increasing steadily. The cost of living continues to
spiral and people live in fear and insecurity. What is
the solution to this sad state of affairs?

There can be only one answer, and that is to confidently place your faith and trust in Jesus Christ. He
conquered a dark and hostile world and replaced
fear with love. He restored hope where circumstances
appeared hopeless. To those who believe in Him, He
gives the blessing of His peace that transcends all understanding.

Believe in Jesus Christ and His promises; place
your trust in Him unconditionally and He will lead
you from the darkness into the light of His immeasurable love for humankind. If you do this you will no
longer worry about the future because the peace of
God will protect you always.

Immanuel!
God is with us!

I rejoice in Your promise like one who
finds great spoil. (Psalm 119:162)

When the outlook is bleak, people become disheartened. The world is beset by major problems that cause people to be scared, anxious, and uncertain. Some people fight the good fight by trying to remove obstacles in their own strength, but to no avail. Others crack under the burden.

One of the great joys of the Christian faith is that Jesus promised that He would be with us until the end. He will not forsake us, and He will never fail us. Such a gracious assurance from the almighty God Himself must undoubtedly fill you with new hope. Jesus triumphed over the worst of what man and life could do to Him, and now the triumphant Christ gives you His promise that He will be with you in every situation and under all circumstances in life.

In order to deal effectively with difficult circumstances, it is crucial that you surrender control of your life to Christ. Yield to His sovereignty and faithfully follow His commands. Be sensitive to the guidance of the Holy Spirit, and He will transform your despair into hope, your depression into a celebration!

ETERNAL LIFE

*For this very reason, Christ died and returned
to life so that He might be the Lord of both
the dead and the living. (Romans 14:9)*

A child leaving home for school; a person changing jobs; the loss of a life partner can leave you with feelings of uncertainty and apprehension. They cause you to fear what the future holds for you.

There are many people who brood over the unknown. In their uncertainty they fall prey to anxiety and tension. They also worry about the dark, unknown future that will follow their physical death.

For the Christian believer there is a glorious truth that emanates from the life, death, and resurrection of Jesus Christ. We know that in the Spirit, He is with us right now to lead us through life with all its problems and fears. He also went to prepare a place for us in God's heavenly kingdom. In this way He assures us that when our earthly life is over, we will be with the Lord forever (John 14:1-4).

Instead of being consumed with fear and worry, hold on to the promises of Jesus Christ. Place your faith and trust in Him and rejoice in the fact that because Jesus lives, you too will live forever.

FOR THOSE HUMDRUM-DAYS

"The thief comes only to steal and kill and destroy;
I have come that they may have life,
and have it to the full." (John 10:10)

When one drab, humdrum day follows the next with tedious monotony and it seems as if your life has no meaning or purpose, it is easy to develop the attitude that nothing in life is worthwhile. Life must have purpose if you are to live meaningfully.

Maybe you have been doing the same work for years and, as far as you can see, you will be doing it for many years to come. What, you may justifiably ask, is the use of thinking that circumstances will change? You feel as if you are trapped in a dead-end street from which you will never be able to escape.

Accepting Christ into your heart changes your attitude toward life. Christ plants new hope in your heart, and dejection and despair begin to dissipate. When you truly start living in Christ, you look at life with new eyes of understanding.

When the powerful teachings of Christ fill you and the Holy Spirit's strength saturates your spirit, life becomes rich and meaningful, and you will find purpose in every day.

GOD IS WITH YOU

"The LORD your God is with you, He is mighty to save.
He will take great delight in you, He will quiet you
with His love, He will rejoice over you
with singing." (Zephaniah 3:17)

When things start going wrong it is easy to despair. Life seems so unfair. Many people who at first seem invincible, simply allow themselves to be overwhelmed by a spirit of helplessness and hopelessness.

If ever everything seemed hopeless, it was on the day of Jesus' crucifixion. The hopes and dreams of those who thought that He was the promised Messiah, sent to set the nation of Israel free, were shattered when He died like a common criminal on the cross.

But then God intervened. The Lord God, who was Christ's hope and strength, miraculously turned apparent defeat into victory. The sorrowful Good Friday was transformed into the triumphant resurrection of Easter Sunday when Christ rose victoriously from the grave.

Whatever circumstances you find yourself in, however dismal the future may seem, and despite all the problems that confront you, always remember that God is with you and that He is in control of your circumstances. Place your faith and trust in Him and He will give you the victory.

GOD'S SILENCE

Yet when He [Jesus] heard that Lazarus was sick, He stayed where He was two more days. (John 11:6)

There are many devout Christians who, like Peter, constantly want to remain on the mountaintop with Jesus. When they occasionally become despondent, they feel that they have somehow disappointed God. The Christian life is lived by ordinary people who are subject to the vagaries of the human heart in which the joys of the mountaintop may be followed by a plunge into the valley of despair. Although we tend to link our spiritual peaks to the presence of God, and our depths to His absence, this is not necessarily true.

Whatever your changing moods, God remains unchangeable. When you are in the depths of despair ask, "What is God wanting to teach me in this situation?"

Many Christians have found that God's will became known to them when they were struggling through the dark valleys. Become still in the midst of your sorrow and self-pity and try to understand God's will for your life. Do not fear when God is silent and appears to be distant. He is just as close to you then as when you were with Him on the mountaintop.

I IN HIM AND HE IN ME

"Remain in Me, and I will remain in you. No branch can bear fruit by itself; it must remain in the vine." (John 15:4)

It is a sad truth that many people who are inspired by Jesus become ardent social reformers or establish political parties. They call themselves Christians and perform many good deeds in His name, yet forget the Source of inspiration. Attempting to serve the Lord without the strength that He alone provides leads to frustration and disappointment.

All true Christians should cultivate an awareness of the living reality of Jesus Christ in their lives. This creates a new awareness of the meaning of life. It helps you see the problems, challenges, joys, and sorrows of your life from His perspective.

The crux of your spiritual life is to know Him as a living reality. Knowing this will affect the way you live each day. Meeting Christ in the silence of solitude and experiencing the touch of His Spirit in your spirit can have far-reaching consequences for your life. Your soul will be wonderfully enriched. To separate such a glorious experience from your day-to-day life could keep you from growing spiritually.

SOMETHING TO LIVE FOR

*"Before long, the world will not see Me
anymore, but you will see Me. Because I live,
you also will live." (John 14:19)*

Many people harbor anxiety over an unknown future and become pessimistic and discouraged. We
must, therefore, constantly remind ourselves that life
is extremely precious, something that even the most
despairing person realizes when his life is threatened.

Even if the future seems bleak, you can be assured
that your life and future are in God's hands. God is
in control of every situation in which you find yourself. He knows your needs and will provide for you
through the abundance of life in Jesus Christ.

As your faith grows stronger, and as you start
trusting Him more, you will begin to realize the joy of
a life in Christ and how trustworthy God is. He is the
Rock upon which you can build your life because His
grace is sufficient to get you through each day.

Through His death and resurrection, Jesus not
only gave you life, but also a reason to live. Through
His Holy Spirit He provides you with the ability to
live life to the fullest. Seize this life and live it in the
abundance of Jesus Christ your Lord.

POSITIVE THINKING – PLUS!

Do not conform any longer to the pattern of this world, but be transformed by the renewing of your mind. Then you will be able to test and approve what God's will is – His good, pleasing and perfect will. (Romans 12:2)

While we recognize the importance of positive thinking, we should also remember that many who preach and practice it are not Christians, even though they use this technique to achieve all kinds of personal goals.

The doctrine of our Lord and Master, Jesus Christ, embraces positive thinking but reaches beyond thoughts to touch the hidden possibilities of the spirit. When we face the reality of situations in our lives, positive thinking can help up to a point, but a relationship with the living Christ can do so much more. Positive thinking can bring about only limited solutions. Real change comes when you move past thinking to an unshakeable trust of Christ's work in your life. He makes all things possible.

Christ gives us the Holy Spirit who enables us to conquer the forces that try to weaken us intellectually and spiritually. Positive thinking together with solid faith in the almighty Christ is a creative force that enables you to live as God intended you to live: in victory and with joy.

CHRIST LIVES!
HE IS ALIVE!

*"Look at My hands and My feet. It is I Myself!
Touch Me and see." (Luke 24:39)*

The triumphant living Christ stands at the center of the Christian faith. This is not a theological debate but an irrefutable fact. Remove the living Christ from the Christian faith and all that is left is a noble-sounding philosophy stripped of all power to change lives. Christ Himself gives power, purpose, and meaning to each generation of believers.

Because Christ rose from the dead and is alive, His teachings are not empty theories but powerful practicalities. Millions of people experience the power of His living presence in their lives and trust in His almighty strength to fill their lives with purpose and meaning.

To partake of this power requires a simple act of childlike faith. Believe, with your whole heart, mind, soul and being that Christ is alive, and that when you surrender to Him He comes to live in you so that He can reveal Himself through you to the world in which you live. As you live in the reality of the knowledge of the resurrection, your life will take on a new dimension of excitement and strength.

MEDITATE ON NOBLE THINGS

*Whatever is true, whatever is noble, whatever is right,
whatever is pure, whatever is lovely, whatever is
admirable—if anything is excellent or praiseworthy—think
about such things. (Philippians 4:8)*

It is all too easy to allow the sordidness of life to taint your personality. Because we live in a world where the accepted norms are not the standards of God, it is tempting to set lower spiritual goals that conform to popular opinion. But then you no longer experience the joy and strength of the indwelling Christ.

It requires spiritual sensitivity to consistently appreciate the beauty of life. Begin by looking for the beautiful and noble acts of Creator God in unexpected places: the smile of a friend, the innocence of a child, an inconspicuous act of love, the success of someone who has struggled for a long time ... In numerous ways you will begin to be aware of the wonder and beauty of life.

One of the greatest gifts is when, through the grace of God, you develop the ability to distinguish between that which is base and offensive, and that which is noble and beautiful. In choosing Christ you open your life to beauty, nobility and truth.

BREAK THE TIES
OF BONDAGE

It is for freedom that Christ has set us free. Stand firm,
then, and do not let yourselves be burdened again
by a yoke of slavery. (Galatians 5:1)

The greatest gift a slave could ever receive was unconditional freedom. To be freed from the ties of bondage brought great joy and delight. You can be certain that, after all the suffering and humiliation, the slave would have done everything in his power not to become a slave again.

There are very few people who have not fallen prey, at one time or another, to the bondage of some form of slavery. People become slaves to habits that are not beneficial to their overall well-being. There are those to whom wealth and status are of the utmost importance. Some people become addicted to drugs or alcohol, with disastrous consequences. Anything that becomes an obsession and has a hold on you reduces you to the status of a slave.

The living Christ, through His great sacrifice of love, offers you true freedom together with abundant life. You must simply accept and embrace Him as your personal Savior and make Him an integral part of your life. Can you afford to refuse His offer?

FREEDOM HAS RESPONSIBILITY

Live as free men, but do not use your freedom as a cover-up for evil; live as servants of God. (1 Peter 2:16)

Freedom is a much-abused word. It is used to rouse people to rebellion, and heinous crimes are committed in its name. Those who follow false leaders promising freedom usually find themselves trapped in a new form of slavery.

True freedom can only be experienced if the human spirit is liberated from hate, meanness, and envy because true freedom is spiritual in nature and can only be known by those who love and serve God.

The vast majority of people live in slavery, even though they may be unaware of the fetters that bind them. Their preconceived ideas and false thought patterns are reflected in their negative attitudes, irascible tempers, hate, and bitterness.

The message of the Christian gospel brings freedom for everyone who is held captive by the destructive influences that control their souls. The living Christ forgives our sins and frees us from the shackles of the evil one.

As you experience the blessing of God's deliverance, you will be transformed into a new, free person, who lives in harmony, peace, and love with God and your fellow human beings.

SET FREE BY
THE HOLY SPIRIT

*Where the Spirit of the Lord is, there
is freedom. (2 Corinthians 3:17)*

Have you ever felt that you are able to achieve more than you do presently and that you are not nearly reaching your full potential? Your life is probably being suffocated by trivialities that deplete all rightful ambition within you.

Even though you may experience a stirring in your spirit every now and then, it is not strong enough to launch you into positive, creative action.

It is a tragedy to continue in a mediocre existence when the Holy Spirit offers you liberty in Christ. When you allow the Holy Spirit to come into your life and take control, you can expect some radical changes. Those inhibitions that prohibited you from living life to the full will start to vanish. In practicing this newfound freedom, you will become aware of the needs of others and you will start living a life of unselfish service.

Suddenly there will be meaning and purpose in your life and you will be empowered to live a life of real and indescribable freedom.

Your traveling companion, the Holy Spirit, is not only your guide, but also the One who protects and inspires you!

THE SECOND COMING OF CHRIST

The end of all things is near. Therefore be clear minded and self-controlled so that you can pray. (1 Peter 4:7)

For centuries people have been trying to determine the exact date on which the world will end. Even though Jesus expressly told us that it is not for us to know the time, the predictions just seem to continue.

The actual date is of little importance if you are equipped and ready to meet Christ. The most important aspect of the Second Coming is not when it will take place, but whether you will be prepared to meet your Lord and to give account for your life and deeds.

People are diligent about earthly matters. They make provision for their retirement; when a storm looms they close the doors and windows; farmers protect their livestock from the cold of winter; we insure ourselves against possible loss in the event of theft, loss, and accidents.

How much more important is it, then, to prepare yourself spiritually so that you can joyfully anticipate the Second Coming of Christ? Discipline yourself to spend time in prayer and meditation in the presence of the Lord; surrender yourself to the leading of the Holy Spirit, so that you will be ready whenever He comes.

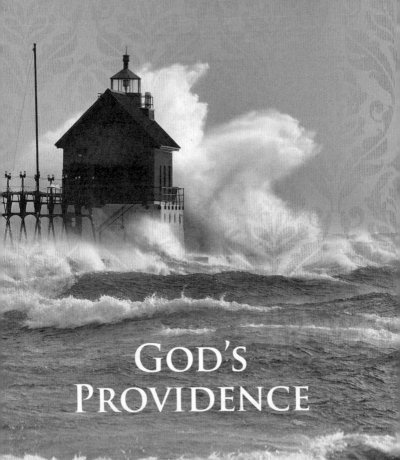

FEBRUARY

GOD'S PROVIDENCE

A CHILD
OF ROYAL BLOOD

You are all sons of God through faith in Christ Jesus, for all of you who were baptized into Christ have clothed yourselves with Christ. (Galatians 3:26-27)

You need never feel spiritually inferior. Perhaps you see how others are asked to be involved in church activities while you are passed over. Your friends are bubbling over with the joy of Christ, while your Christian walk seems drab and uneventful. In prayer and study groups other people speak and pray, but you keep quiet. Others know so much about the Bible that it leaves you feeling guilty and inadequate.

Remember that when God accepted you as His child He did not do so on the basis of your knowledge, work, or worthiness. It depended entirely on your faith in Jesus Christ and your acceptance of Him as your Redeemer and Savior.

Jesus accepts you for who and what you are. All He asks is that you believe in Him and accept Him as the Lord of your life. In the Gospel of John, Jesus says, "Do not let your hearts be troubled. Trust in God; trust also in Me" (John 14:1).

Joyfully respond to this invitation and experience the grace and love of your divine Father every day.

All-surrounding love

*"I am the good shepherd. The good shepherd
lays down His life for the sheep." (John 10:11)*

Sheep and goats were very precious livestock to the
Palestinian shepherds. They provided most of what
the people needed for their livelihood and well-being.
The shepherd took special care of them by leading
them to pastures and water, by protecting them, by
keeping them on the right path, and by searching for
the ones that went astray.

Jesus calls Himself the good Shepherd who cares
for God's precious children. He provides for your
daily needs, protects you, shows you the path of righteousness, and searches for you when you go astray.
Then He lovingly brings you back to the safety of the
flock.

However, there is one crucial difference between
the Palestinian shepherd and his flock, and the good
Shepherd and His children. In order to enjoy the care
and protection of the shepherd, the flock had to provide for the needs of the people. Jesus Christ, the
good Shepherd, however, offers you His protection
and immeasurable love, and asks only that you love
Him in return. Is this too high a price to pay for a love
that exceeds all other loves by far?

GOD PROTECTS HIS LABORERS

Being confident of this, that He who began a good work in you will carry it on to completion until the day of Christ Jesus. (Philippians 1:6)

In every generation, followers of Jesus Christ do His will whole-heartedly. Some of them are in prominent positions in society; others are not very well known, but regardless of their status, their zeal and love for the Lord challenges and motivates their fellow believers.

Spiritual giants tend to have had vivid and unique experiences with their Savior. Paul never forgot his experience on the road to Damascus; Brother Lawrence loved being in his kitchen with Christ; John Wesley felt his "heart to be strangely warmed" in a room in Aldersgate Street in London. Many other disciples also experience the reality of the living Christ in various ways.

The Lord comes to each of His followers in their own unique circumstances, meeting them at their own level and place. Not every true disciple has to have a Damascus Road experience.

As your relationship with Jesus Christ deepens, you will become aware of a divine plan unfolding for your life. Whether it is extraordinary or ordinary, it is God's will and in executing it, you will find joy and a deep satisfaction – as well as His protection.

GOD IS IMMUTABLE

He set the earth on its foundations;
it can never be moved. (Psalm 104:5)

In every aspect of life, from science and mathematics to the way we live our everyday lives, we need to be certain of the things that remain constant in order to experience stability. It is essential to have a set standard on which to base your lifestyle. If this constancy and awareness of an absolute standard is missing, confusion and chaos will result.

The Lord Himself provides us with the consistency that is required for the day-to-day functioning of humanity. He said, "I the LORD do not change" (Mal. 3:6).

People come and go; times change; fads and fashions pass; moral standards, behavior, and principles seem to vary from one generation to the next. If you follow the passing trends of the world, there is a very real danger that you will become confused and find it difficult to know how you should live your life and what exactly is expected of you.

Focus on the Lord to free yourself from doubt and confusion. He set the standard for successful living and if you follow Him your life will be filled with peace and satisfaction.

THE MIGHTY HAND OF GOD

For the wisdom of this world is foolishness in God's sight. (1 Corinthians 3:19)

All through the ages, people have claimed the honor of making the greatest discovery of all time. Think of the wheel, fire, and the power of steam, followed by electricity, the telephone, radio, and television. Great leaps of progress have been made in the spheres of science, mathematics, medicine, atomic and nuclear power, and our computer-based society has radically changed the world we live in.

While we do not disparage the wonders of these discoveries, we should never forget the omnipotence of God in this world of so-called human achievement.

Take a little time to quietly ponder how humanity would have fared without the assistance of the Lord. Just as He created people, He also provided them with knowledge and abilities. The expertise of scientists, engineers, and doctors did not appear out of nothing, but is the result of God-given talent.

Despite all the excitement over human achievement throughout the ages, we must never neglect to notice the mighty hand of God that moves all things in history.

"How great Thou art!"

Come and see what God has done, how awesome
His works in man's behalf! (Psalm 66:5)

Many people find very little that is good or worthwhile in the world. They resign themselves to what
seems to be a hopeless future. They are blinded to
the glory and greatness of God because they put their
trust in men and the way they govern the world.

To approach life with courage and steadfastness,
and to ensure tranquility of mind and inner peace, you
need to constantly remind yourself of the wonderful
deeds God has performed in your life.

Meditate on the beauty of creation; consider all the
daily blessings that you often take for granted but that
enrich your life; think of the riches of good health;
and marvel at the fellowship of family and friends.
And above all this, meditate again on the comforting
and strengthening presence of the living Savior.

When you are tempted to regard this life as a failure, praise and glorify God for the awesome wonder of life. Praise will lift you above the things that
are wrong with the world and open your eyes to the
majesty and greatness of the omnipotent Creator of
heaven and earth.

Know God's Grace
and Live!

Grace and peace be yours in abundance. (1 Peter 1:2)

More and more people are searching for the ability to handle the problems of our day with peace of mind. Life has become extremely complicated for many, with all kinds of traps and obstacles along the way.

People tend to seek man-made methods to handle their problems. Temporary solutions such as alcohol and drugs provide a brief refuge that helps to block out reality for a while. But the problem does not just disappear. In fact, the physical and mental ability to handle problems diminishes and they end up feeling discouraged, and burdened with guilt and self-reproach.

There is only one sure method of handling your life with confidence and assurance, and that is in the power of Jesus Christ. If you commit yourself and your life to Him unconditionally, then you can rest assured that He will give you the grace required to handle every problem. You will thus be blessed with tranquility of mind and peace far beyond human understanding.

This grace and peace become a reality in your life only through Jesus Christ. Don't drift from Him and so forfeit what only He can give.

YOUR FAITHFUL SAVIOR

Because of the LORD's great love we are not consumed,
for His compassions never fail. (Lamentations 3:22)

There are many times in our lives when everything seems hopeless and lost. We fall ill; adversity descends upon us; fear overwhelms us; or we experience the pain of death's final separation. These things leave us feeling a loneliness that borders on despair. What can we do in such circumstances and how do we cope with life?

Some people are extremely blessed to experience the support of their family and friends in such times. But even though you may have people who gather around you, eventually even that support falls away, because they also have their own lives to live and their own families to care for.

When life plunges you into some or other crisis, you should not forget the goodness and faithfulness of God. You are His child, whom He has chosen, and in His Word, He reassures you time and again of His continual presence. The living Christ is at your side at all times and in every circumstance. He will guide you from the darkness of despair into His wonderful light of hope and peace. Walk with Him and be filled with His love and peace.

BROADEN YOUR VISION OF GOD

"How great is God–beyond our understanding!" (Job 36:26)

One obstacle to our spiritual growth is our limited concept of God. You may believe that God loves and cares for you. You acknowledge that He is all-powerful, all-knowing, and omnipresent. But as soon as disaster threatens, you relegate God to the backseat. Your fail to draw on the wisdom and strength that He has placed at your disposal. Your problems appear bigger than your concept of God.

Broaden your vision of God when things are going well. Spend more time in your private devotions, and expand your interest in the world around you. Increase your awareness of the greatness of God, and use all the elements of His grace to get to know Him more intimately.

When the inevitable storms start looming, you will find that you possess spiritual reserves that will enable you to be strong, regardless of how difficult your circumstances are.

The greater your understanding of God, the more strength you will draw from Him in moments of temptation. Your faith will no longer be an emotional response, but a knowledge of God Himself.

"I KNOW FOR CERTAIN!"

*The LORD is my shepherd, I shall
not be in want. (Psalm 23:1)*

Those of us who belong to the Lord know we are safe and secure. We know for certain that the Lord is our Shepherd and therefore we do not fear the future. Our Shepherd is there already and He will walk before us every day, leading us to our eternal destination.

Do you feel unsure about the path you have to take? Remember, He is the Good Shepherd. Whether you turn to the right or to the left, your ears will hear a voice behind you, saying, "This is the way; walk in it" (Isa. 30:21).

Do you need spiritual food and strength? The Lord will provide an abundant feast of good things. He is our heavenly manna, the bread and water of life.

Sometimes we have doubts about the future. We wonder whether we will have enough to provide for our essential needs. With childlike certainty, the psalmist then tells us, "I shall not be in want." I shall not be "in want" of anything that I truly need and that is good for me. The Lord will hear when you call, because His love never changes.

PEACE AND PROSPERITY

You will keep in perfect peace him whose mind is steadfast, because he trusts in You. (Isaiah 26:3)

When our minds are focused on the love of God, we experience indescribable tranquility and peace of mind. It is not in vain that the Lord promised, "Peace I leave with you; My peace I give you. I do not give to you as the world gives. Do not let your hearts be troubled and do not be afraid" (John 14:27).

When you trust God through every day and every sleepless night, you will not only experience peace of mind, but you will also stop worrying about the well-being and prosperity of your loved ones, because you know that they are safe in God's loving care.

By focusing on Jesus Christ and the peace and prosperity that He gives, you are set free from worry because you know God is in control of your life. Then no person or circumstance can disturb your tranquility.

He sets you free from anxious worry and tension. His love enfolds you, and it covers your loved ones as well. This freedom cannot be taken away by anyone or anything – simply because you put your trust in the Lord.

LIFE-ALTERING LIGHT

*"Can His forces be numbered? Upon whom
does His light not rise?" (Job 25:3)*

It is wonderful how beauty can be experienced in the most unlikely places. The rays of the rising or setting sun transfigure an arid desert landscape. Steep gorges lose their austerity when the light of the rising moon illuminates them. Barren lands are transformed, almost overnight, into a wonderland of color after the spring rains have fallen on the apparently dead earth.

All of these reveal God's omnipotence as He cares for His creation. He proves in so many ways that all things are possible for Him. In the same way that, in the very beginning, He created light from the darkness, so He can still today transform the darkest night into dazzling morning light.

His divine wonders are not limited to nature. Jesus also moves in the lives of people, and will bring light to your darkness if you are willing to turn to Him and trust Him.

In spite of your circumstances you can be sure that the living Christ is prepared to lead you from the darkness of your circumstances into the wonderful light of the presence of God.

GOD IS IN CONTROL

*Then Job replied to the LORD: "I know that You
can do all things; no plan of Yours can
be thwarted." (Job 42:1-2)*

The world is filled with pessimists who find little
that is right with this world. They see no hope for the
future and spread gloom and dejection wherever they
go. Their constant negativity causes them to become
mean-spirited and cynical.

Take a few minutes to meditate on the greatness of
God. You will find many examples of the wonderful
ways in which God transforms despair into hope; sorrow into joy; and defeat into victory.

Of all these examples, the one that rises above all
the others is the way in which God used the horror
of Jesus' crucifixion to reveal the wonder of His forgiving love in the glory of the resurrection. To those
of little faith, Golgotha was the end of a sorrowful
road, but Easter Sunday ushered in the beginning of
a wonderful new life: God's plan for the redemption
of mankind had been completed.

When things around you appear dark and terrify-
ing, hold on to the promises of God. Remember the
mighty deeds that He has done, and confidently go
forward with the certain knowledge that He is completely in control.

A GOD WHO ENCOURAGES

May the God who gives endurance and encouragement
give you a spirit of unity among yourselves as
you follow Christ Jesus. (Romans 15:5)

We all experience times when depression pulls us down. For no apparent reason you cannot handle the demands of life any more. Everything you try seems to fail; you become discouraged and feel that you are no longer able to cope with life.

When you've come to the end of your own abilities, it is good to become silent before God and receive the encouragement that only He can give. Submit yourself to Him and receive His hope. Otherwise the old familiar despair will take hold of you again.

In the silent awareness of God's divine presence, recall His glorious promises. That will revive hope in your soul. Reassure yourself that both in the storm and the quiet, God, in Christ Jesus, is with you. Remember that He promised to make all things new. He will give you the strength to complete the task that He has given you to do.

God does not want you to remain permanently in the dark valley of despair. He will give you the encouragement that will make your life meaningful and beautiful again.

DIVINE PROTECTION

They remembered that God was their Rock, that
God Most High was their Redeemer. (Psalm 78:35)

Many times in the history of the world it seemed as if all was lost and all hope gone. People, and even nations, were forced to admit defeat in a battle against the superior numbers of the enemy.

But there have been even more cases in which people and nations were delivered in answer to their prayers. God has saved people and nations from devastation in miraculous ways, and has enabled them to overcome dangers and transform humiliating defeat into glorious victory.

These cases, both personal and historical, should serve as a constant reminder of the victorious omnipotence of God in all spheres of life. No circumstances are too small or too big for Him, and no prayer will remain unheard or unanswered. This is the extent of God's immeasurable love for His people and His world.

Where adverse circumstances threaten to overwhelm you, or fear makes your heart tremble, remember that Christ sacrificed His life for you. Turn to Him and lay your fears at His feet, because only in Him will you find deliverance from your distress.

GOD IS INFALLIBLE

Where is the wise man? Where is the scholar? Where is the philosopher of this age? Has not God made foolish the wisdom of the world? (1 Corinthians 1:20)

In spite of all the progress humankind has made in the fields of science and technology, people are living with more stress and tension than ever before. In spite of all that has been achieved, a restlessness haunts both young and old. It seems that the entire human race is caught up in the uncertainties of the present and fear of the future.

Only when you acknowledge the all-sufficiency of God will you be able to begin to live life fully. When we are bound by the drudgery and tragic results of the so-called progress that has been made, we find no rest for our souls. We are caught up in a modern version of slavery.

True peace of mind is found only in a relationship with Jesus Christ. Unless you put your trust in Him unconditionally, allowing Him to direct the course of your life, you will never be rid of the destructive power of guilt and fear.

In Christ you will find the ability to achieve the goals that He has planned for you, and your heart will be filled with peace.

GOD IS WITH YOU

"You are the God who sees me," for she said, "I have now seen the One who sees me." (Genesis 16:13)

The question on everybody's lips is, "Who is God? What is He really like?" Some people try to use their imaginations to depict the Almighty. Some even claim to have seen Him in visions. Others, however, feel that because we are unable to see Him, He doesn't even exist.

Jesus Christ told His followers that no one except the Son has seen the Father. He also told them that no one could come to the Father except through the Son. It therefore follows that you find the Father when you first seek Jesus.

Knowing Jesus requires you to fully surrender and commit your life to Him. And as you become more involved in His service, you will become increasingly aware of His presence. When you visit ill, lonely, and grieving people, you will find Him there.

Because Jesus is in the Father and the Father is in Him, every act of grace, every little bit of compassion, every smidgen of love that you show to others in the name of Jesus, will bring you face to face with God in Jesus Christ.

GOD IS IN EVERYDAY THINGS

*In his heart a man plans his course, but the
LORD determines his steps. (Proverbs 16:9)*

God often works in great and miraculous ways. We
see His glory in the changing heavens; His handiwork
in the grandeur of creation. Despite appearances to
the contrary, the earth still belongs to Him and He is
still in control of it.

God is also the Creator of the small and everyday
things: the perfection of the rose; the fragility of the
forget-me-not. All these things reflect a creative God
who is also the Master of order and detail.

We so easily forget that God is interested in our
well-being. Just consider how many times He has
guided you through difficult circumstances. Sometimes He responded in such an ordinary way to your
prayers that you hardly recognized His answer.

When you pray, watch carefully because you never
know how God will answer. Many people continue
praying for things long after God has answered their
prayers. Others see their answered prayers as mere
coincidence.

God chooses His own way of working in your
life and it is often through the everyday and familiar
things in life that He chooses to do so.

GODLY ASSISTANCE

I can do everything through Him who
gives me strength. (Philippians 4:13)

How often have you avoided a task because you thought it was too difficult for you? Many people find their responsibilities too demanding and therefore they refuse to accept the challenge, and so miss out on many wonderful opportunities in life.

As long as you trust in your own abilities, there will always be challenges that you fail, leaving you feeling inadequate and unworthy. This usually has a negative effect on your self-confidence and ability to handle issues and situations that arise.

Remember that when God calls you to do something, He knows that you are the one to complete the task He assigned.

God does not necessarily call those who are able: He enables those whom He calls. In Christ your Lord, God will enable you to do what He has called you to do.

Whatever you are called to do, pray about it, and dedicate your task to Christ. Seek the Holy Spirit's help and obediently and willingly follow wherever He leads you. You will not fail, because God Himself will be with you.

REMEMBER WHO YOU ARE!

So God created man in His own image, in the image of God He created him. (Genesis 1:27)

When it seems as if nothing in your life is working out, it is time to remember a few spiritual facts. You were created in the image of God. Yes, this image has been damaged and perhaps you have forgotten your rich spiritual heritage.

But knowing that you were created in His image should flood your heart and mind with new hope and inspiration. You were not created to be tossed about by capricious moods beyond your control.

Because you have been created in the image of God you have been created for spiritual greatness, and you will know no rest or satisfaction until you live in the awareness of His presence, and so grow and develop spiritually.

If you are afflicted by feelings of inferiority, you can find comfort in remembering that you are a spiritual being created to live in the holy presence of the Lord. You will find freedom in drawing on the abundance of God's strength. Then you will live life confidently, knowing that His Spirit is working in you.

THE LIVING CHRIST IS REAL

The Spirit Himself testifies with our spirit that we are God's children. (Romans 8:16)

Your ultimate goal should be to know and experience the living Christ in your life. Without Him you may maintain a high moral standard, but it will lack the spiritual dynamism and power that are essential elements of a living faith.

Jesus Christ is much more than a historical figure. He is the inspiration and driving force of millions of powerful lives in the world today. It is not enough to recognize only the Christ of history: what you really need is an awareness of His living presence at this moment in your life. This awareness will never become a reality until you develop a passionate longing to make Him your own. A half-hearted desire is simply not enough.

When your greatest passion is to experience the presence of Christ, you will speak to Him from the silence of your heart; share with Him the things that are happening to you.

If there have been moments when you excluded Him from your life, tell Him that you are sorry, and you will find that His grace enables you to restore your relationship with Him.

OMNIPOTENT PROTECTOR

*"The LORD is my rock, my fortress and my deliverer;
my God is my rock, in whom I take refuge, my shield
and the horn of my salvation. He is my stronghold,
my refuge, and my savior." (2 Samuel 22:2-3)*

When we are afflicted and needy, the love and omnipotence of God protect us. We can overcome any challenge, adversity, or problem if we only steadfastly trust in His loving care and grace.

He will command His angels to watch over us and protect us from any danger. We will not be overwhelmed by evil and left powerless. The ability He gives us to choose, in His light, between what is good and right and what is wrong and unprofitable, will help us to act wisely.

Our ability to think and react quickly and then to act wisely is our protection against unexpected attacks and temptations from Satan. Our ability to adapt to our circumstances, to always have a song in our hearts, and to be joyful, regardless of the situation, protects us against loneliness and depression.

Through the love that is in our hearts, we give and receive love. Then peace and joy fill our minds and hearts, and we are assured that we have an omnipotent Protector.

COMFORT FOR THE FUTURE

"Now the dwelling of God is with men, and He will live with them. They will be His people, and God Himself will be with them and be their God." (Revelation 21:3)

Fear casts a very dark shadow over the future. All over the world clashes between nations and leaders cause people to wonder what kind of world our children and grandchildren will inherit.

When you find refuge in the living Christ your perspective rises above the temporal, and you find a new ability to appreciate the beauty of life. You realize that regardless of how ominous things might appear, everything is still under God's control. The Lord God Almighty still reigns and has not abandoned His creation.

If you believe in the omnipotence of God and if your faith is built on a solid foundation, you will approach life with a positive attitude. To believe that God is working out His divine plan in spite of man's sinfulness, enables you to maintain a well-balanced and calm attitude. You can look to the future without God and experience depression and fear, or you can believe in God's plan of redemption for mankind and approach the future with trust and confidence.

GRACE INDESCRIBABLY GREAT

"My grace is sufficient for you, for My power is made perfect in weakness." (2 Corinthians 12:9)

People often find themselves in situations that make them feel incompetent and inadequate. The magnitude of the situation or the responsibility attached to it, its possible consequences in your own life or in the lives of others, all weigh heavily upon you and so you avoid the responsibility as much as possible.

When you find yourself in such circumstances, do not rely on your own abilities. Jesus made it very clear that we are capable of doing nothing without Him, but that with Him we can do anything that needs to be done. In this truth lies the answer to all your fears, doubts, and insecurities.

Whatever you do in your life, first take it to God in prayer and lay all your expectations, fears, and concerns before Him. Jesus is your Friend, and in the same way that you consult another person before making a decision, you can seek Christ's help in prayer.

By allowing Him to work through you, you will achieve the kind of success that would be unattainable in your own strength.

GOD'S GREAT OMNIPOTENCE

"As for God, His way is perfect; the word of the
LORD is flawless. He is a shield for all who
take refuge in Him." (2 Samuel 22:31)

Regardless of how hard we try to remain true to our promises, at one time or another we all fall short and are unable to keep them. However, this is not the case with God. At the end of his reign, David glorifies the Lord with the words, "As for God, His way is blameless; the word of the LORD is flawless."

David describes God as a rock, a shield, and a fortress. And God guides His people onto higher heights like fleet-footed deer. These images all imply that even though dangers and problems still surround God's children, He provides security in the midst of all these perils.

Whether you walk in the sun or the shade today, reflect on the trustworthiness of our God and praise and glorify Him for being faithful to His promises.

PRAISE FOR GOD'S GRANDEUR

Among the gods there is none like You, O LORD; no deeds can compare with Yours. All the nations You have made will come and worship before You, O LORD; they will bring glory to Your name. (Psalm 86:8-9)

Sometimes our prayers are so focused on danger and affliction, that we forget that we are praying to the almighty and awesome God.

David had a different attitude when he prayed. He realized that his God was greater than all the other pagan gods, and that his God had already demonstrated His miraculous power in many ways and on many occasions. David looked forward to the day when all nations, and not only the Israelites, will acknowledge the sovereignty of the Almighty God. He alone is God!

Let us lift our eyes past the problems that we notice all around us, and let us look toward the Eternal and Triumphant King. Cast the problems that are causing you concern upon your miraculous God. He will care for you.

GOD'S GRACE
IS SUFFICIENT

The days of the blameless are known to the LORD, and their inheritance will endure forever. (Psalm 37:18)

We often hear of people who apparently live virtuous lives and yet are plagued by disaster. They live frugally and make provision for their future, and then, through no fault of their own, they are struck by disaster and face financial ruin. There are those who generously give of themselves in the loving and compassionate care of others, and then find themselves or a loved one struck by illness or death.

When such things happen to you, it is difficult to agree with Paul when he says, "And we know that in all things God works for the good of those who love Him, who have been called according to His purpose" (Rom. 8:28). The human response is to immediately question God's actions, and to wonder whether it is, in fact, worthwhile to live a virtuous and honorable life.

It is, however, important to remember that God's perspective on life is eternal, and that He truly desires all things to work for your own good. Paul also says that our present suffering does not outweigh the glory that will be revealed in us (Rom. 8:18). Take courage and let your heart be peaceful: God's grace is sufficient!

An open door

*"See, I have placed before you an open door
that no one can shut." (Revelation 3:8)*

Some people complain that life is often empty and meaningless. One dreary hour follows the next, one uninteresting day follows the next, and time drags by while they lead a futile existence. It doesn't take them long to wilt intellectually and to develop a negative, cynical attitude to life.

But Jesus Christ has given to you, and all others, the promise of an abundant life – and the opportunity to experience it to the full (John 10:10). Scripture, history, and your personal experience offer ample testimony to the fact that an ordinary, dull life is transformed by the power of the living Christ and through His Holy Spirit.

Through the wonder of God's grace, sadness is transformed into joy; defeat into victory; fear evaporates; hate melts into love; despair into hope – even death becomes life. The moment you accept Christ into your life as Redeemer and Savior, everything in life gains new meaning and purpose. This new life of abundance that Christ offers you is yours for the taking. Turn to Christ and He will open the door to a new, meaningful life for you.

FIND YOUR STRENGTH IN HIM

Strengthen the feeble hands, steady the knees that give way; say to those with fearful hearts, "Be strong, do not fear; your God will come." (Isaiah 35:3-4)

It is regrettable that many people never realize their full potential because they live in fear and underestimate themselves. They have the ability, but when the time of testing comes, they give up. As a result, they begin to feel inadequate, which in turn increases their feeling of inferiority.

A Christian need never suffer this kind of loss. As a child of God, you have the promise of His Son, Jesus Christ, that He will take your burdens upon Himself and will bear your guilt. He wants to be your inseparable companion through life.

Jesus invites you to come to Him with all your fears, anxieties, and insecurities. You have His Word of promise that He will never leave you nor forsake you (Heb. 13:5).

With the promise of His divine support and the steadfast assurance that the Son of God is with you in every situation, you can move forward in confidence: secure in His Name and unafraid of what may lie ahead. Just as He was in the past, God is in the future as well. Does one need greater encouragement than that?

MARCH

JESUS CHRIST, SON OF GOD

The Man of Sorrows

He was despised and rejected by men, a man of sorrows, and familiar with suffering. (Isaiah 53:3)

Christ's suffering reminds us that God's grace does not come cheap: the price was suffering, sorrow, and the blood of His only Son. The uniqueness of Christ's suffering did not lie so much in His physical suffering even though He endured indescribable agony on the cross. Crucifixion was the most barbaric and merciless of deaths.

C. K. Schilder wrote a trilogy on the suffering of Christ. In his writings the author maintains, "The suffering of His soul was the soul of His suffering." He, the One without sin, in obedience to the Father, became sin for our sakes.

The unbearable burden of the sins of all people through the ages was placed on His shoulders and He carried it to Golgotha on our behalf.

Let us focus on the suffering of Christ until we see ourselves standing alone and individually, helpless and in anguish before God.

THE COMPASSIONATE CHRIST

*When He saw the crowds, He had compassion on them,
because they were harassed and helpless, like sheep
without a shepherd. (Matthew 9:36)*

Compassion is one of the outstanding characteristics of the unique personality of Jesus Christ. His
teachings reveal the depths of His wisdom and the
uniqueness of His person.

The attitude that He revealed when talking to people not only stimulated their minds, but captured
their hearts as well. They felt His love for them and
responded by loving Him in return.

Because the immortal Christ is still alive, His compassion for humankind today is just as real and true as
when He walked the dusty roads of Palestine. When
we read the Gospels, our hearts are gladdened by
the reality of His love for people: He healed the sick,
opened blind eyes and deaf ears, restored crippled
feet to walk again, and even raised the dead.

If you don't know where to turn for strength and
inspiration, then remember the compassion of Jesus
Christ. He is with you in all your distress and encourages you through the power of His love, to get up
from the ashes and start building a new life.

GOD'S REDEEMING LOVE

To them God has chosen to make known among the Gentiles the glorious riches of this mystery, which is Christ in you, the hope of glory. (Colossians 1:27)

The wonder and glory of the Christian gospel is that God loved us while we were yet sinners. Without such a love we would indeed have still been lost. Faith in the saving love of God is much more than a pious theological hope, or a dogmatic point for debate.

As you become deeply aware of your imperfection and sin, you are also aware that there is a divine and all-powerful Deity who is calling you to a better and nobler life.

You know that you will never be able to reach such moral heights in your own strength and you might begin to lose hope, and so neglect to give your spiritual life the attention it deserves.

Once you are aware that, because of your sinfulness, you don't have the ability to live your life as you should, it is important to accept God's offer to recreate and reform your life.

Allow the Holy Spirit to fill you with the strength you need to walk according to God's ways.

JESUS PRAYS FOR HIS DISCIPLES

"Holy Father, protect them by the power of Your name – the name You gave Me – so that they may be one as We are one. While I was with them, I protected them and kept them safe by that name You gave Me." (John 17:11-12)

Just before Jesus was arrested by Roman soldiers, He took time to pray for His disciples. He asked the Father to protect those for whom He would die. Listen to the words of Jesus, "Holy Father, protect them by the power of Your name ... that they may be one as We are one." Jesus' prayer reveals the attitude of His heart. He cares for His disciples and desires for them to live together in unity.

Jesus cares for us, His followers today, just as He cared for His disciples so long ago. Meditate on the wonder of the fact that Jesus cares for you and ask Him to help you to live in peace with your fellow Christians.

CHRIST'S REASSURING PRESENCE

While they were still talking about this, Jesus
Himself stood among them and said to them,
"Peace be with you." (Luke 24:36)

Jesus' disciples were stunned after the terrible events
of that first Good Friday. Without their beloved Master they were scared, confused, and without a leader.
Their dreams had been shattered and life had lost
all meaning for them. Dejected and disheartened,
this sad group were commiserating together – when
suddenly Jesus appeared in their midst.

The transformation in their lives was nothing short
of a miracle. Examples of the powerful deeds that
they performed in the Name of the Master abound
in the Scriptures. The presence of Jesus brought new
impetus and drive to their lives.

All of this happened two thousand years ago, but
the resurrected and living Christ still has the same
impact on the lives of people today.

If you are depressed or disheartened; if you are
in danger of giving up hope; then it is time to invite
Jesus into your life and to ask Him to support you.
Trust Him unconditionally and allow Him to change
your despair into hope and your sadness into joy.

SOMETHING TO LIVE FOR

*"Before long, the world will not see Me
anymore, but you will see Me. Because I live,
you also will live." (John 14:19)*

Despite how gloomy the future may appear, it is vitally important to accept that your life and your future are both in the hands of God. The Christian's life is not ruled by blind fate. God is in control of every situation in which you find yourself. He knows your needs and is willing to provide for you through the wealth and abundance of Jesus Christ.

As your faith grows and becomes stronger, and as you start trusting Him more and more, you will also begin to realize how great the joy of a life in Christ is and how trustworthy God is. He is the Rock upon which you can build your entire life and future, knowing that His grace is enough to get you through each day.

Through His death and resurrection, Jesus not only gave you life, but also a reason to live. Through His Holy Spirit He also provides you with the ability to live life to the fullest. Seize this life and live it in the abundance of Jesus Christ your Lord.

CHRIST
UNLOCKS ETERNITY

Now we see but a poor reflection as in a mirror; then
we shall see face to face. Now I know in part;
then I shall know fully, even as I am fully
known. (1 Corinthians 13:12)

If we could reach God only through knowledge and argument, the learned and gifted would be the only people to find Him. But God made the path leading to Him a 'Via Regium' – a kingly highroad" (Lancelot Andrewes). Christ opens the way to new vistas for us on this highroad to God.

We do not know what the future holds, but we do know the One who has the future in His mighty hand. We do not know the way, but we know Jesus who opens the way. Even though we cannot answer all of life's questions, we know that Jesus Christ is God's answer.

If we want to receive God's gifts of forgiveness and eternal life we should step out onto the unknown road with confidence and faith in Jesus Christ. Speak to God about your doubts and your pain and accept the sovereignty of Christ in every situation in your life.

One day we will come face to face with the Savior. We will know Him as He knows us and we will find the answers.

INTEGRATE GOD IN YOUR LIFE

*"Remain in Me, and I will remain in you.
No branch can bear fruit by itself; it must
remain in the vine." (John 15:4)*

It is sad that many people call themselves Christians and perform many good deeds in His name, and yet forget the Person who called them to know and serve Him. Attempting to serve the Lord without the strength that He alone can provide inevitably leads to frustration and disappointment.

Every faithful believer should cultivate the glorious truth that Jesus Christ is a living Person until His presence becomes a reality in our daily lives. By becoming aware of His presence, you begin to see the problems, challenges, joys, and sorrows of your existence from His perspective and He becomes a more integral part of your life.

The essence of your spiritual life is to know Him as a living reality. Meeting Christ in the silence of solitude and experiencing the touch of His Spirit on your spirit has far-reaching consequences for your life. Your soul is truly enriched and to deny yourself such an experience can lead to spiritual emptiness.

Only Jesus

*When they looked up, they saw no
one except Jesus. (Matthew 17:8)*

Perhaps it is time to pause for a moment and examine
your spiritual pilgrimage under the leadership and
guidance of the Holy Spirit. Put all preconceived
ideas aside and open up your spirit for His guidance.

If you allow the Holy Spirit to work freely in your
life, He will lead you into a deeper and more intimate
relationship with the living Christ. Jesus will begin to
occupy the central position in your life – a position
He cannot and will not share with anyone else.

It is the all-important sovereignty of Jesus Christ
that generates a living faith in our hearts. Everything
that glorifies Him is inspired by the Spirit of the living
God. Any doctrine that does not give Christ precedence is not from God.

Faith is powerless and meaningless unless it is
grounded in Christ. Only when He truly rules as
King in your life and heart will your faith be alive
and meaningful. No one except Jesus – this is the call
of the human heart.

CHRIST ALONE

For I resolved to know nothing while I was with you except Jesus Christ and Him crucified. (1 Corinthians 2:2)

To know Christ as Lord and Master and to worship Him as the perfect revelation of God are truly enriching experiences. The way that you encounter Christ will be unique to you but you must guard against confusing the path you took to find Christ with Christ Himself. The Christian path is in a certain sense also a very wide path, wide enough to include the extremes of genuine Christian experience.

Whether you follow the path of the fundamentalist or the orthodox or the charismatic is not an issue. What truly matters is the common purpose: to glorify God through the living and risen Christ.

If you allow yourself to be thrown onto a side track through methods and theories and lose sight of Christ, you lose the core part of your Christianity.

Living faith is founded on a personal experience of the risen Christ and not on theories and speculations about Him. You need only worship Him and glorify Him and live surrounded by His love. Then your doctrine and testimony will be sound.

THE INVISIBLE PARTNER

"And surely I am with you always, to the very end of the age." (Matthew 28:20)

Christ is the inspiration and source of a positive approach to life. It is only possible to be aware of His living presence if He occupies the place of honor in your life. Without that, you will never experience the wonder and joy that His presence can bring to your life. To know Him you need to spend quality time with Him.

Speak to Him as to a trusted and loved Friend. If you unburden your heart and mind to Him, you receive not only peace and deliverance, but also find the bond of love between you strengthened.

Talking to the living Christ before the bustle of the day starts, develops a relationship that will greatly influence your thoughts and actions throughout the day.

The wisdom and strength you find in your quiet time with Him increases as you focus on His holy and blessed presence. Even brief prayers during the day can keep you in touch with Him. Then you will truly live victoriously in His holy presence.

TRUE LOVE

Love must be sincere. (Romans 12:9)

The word *love* is probably the most used and least understood word in any language. It has been used about art, food, and leisure time activities. It is even used in connection with clothes and cars.

When you tell people that you love them, it would be beneficial to consider the actual depth of your love. To what lengths would you go and what sacrifices would you be willing to make for the sake of love?

Jesus Christ came to demonstrate the meaning of true love when He willingly gave His life for all of humanity. He was willing to die for all of us and to take our punishment upon Himself to redeem us from our sinfulness. As He said, "Greater love has no one than this, that He lay down His life for His friends" (John 15:13).

True love involves making sacrifices for the sake of another. It is tolerant, patient, and understanding, even in the most trying circumstances. It involves forgiveness and giving of yourself for the benefit of others. It means to love others as Jesus loves you.

Unchanging Rock of Ages

Jesus Christ is the same yesterday and today and forever. (Hebrews 13:8)

It is only natural for us to picture Jesus Christ as a Jew who lived during the golden age of the Roman Empire. It was during that time that God chose to reveal Himself to the world through His Son. And so we easily lose sight of the eternal existence and unchanging quality of Christ.

He is eternal and therefore He lives today! Just as He taught, guided, and blessed His first disciples, He wants to do the same for you today. Unfortunately our perspective on His ability to help us and to bless us is clouded by the problems and confusion of our modern society. But the basic problems of the world today are exactly the same as when Jesus was on earth.

Greed, lust, self-centeredness, pettiness, hate, and bitterness are still powerful influences in the lives of men and women.

The living Christ can deal with these negative aspects of the human heart and mind – just as He could centuries ago, because He is eternal and unchanging. On this steadfast Rock we can build our lives.

JESUS IS TRULY HUMAN

Many deceivers, who do not acknowledge Jesus Christ as coming in the flesh, have gone out into the world. Any such person is the deceiver and the antichrist. (2 John 1:7)

It is fundamental to the Christian faith that Jesus Christ was born as a human being, lived, died, and was buried, and that He was resurrected from the dead and ascended into heaven. If this was not so, the Lord we worship would have remained completely inaccessible to ordinary people.

God, in His infinite wisdom and love for the world, took on human form and came to live as a man among humans. He shared in their joy and sorrow and suffered the same pain and emotions that they did. Therefore, Jesus understands people and life – the good as well as the bad. If God had not taken on human form we would never have known the dynamic impact of Jesus Christ on our lives, and people would still be walking in darkness.

It is now your responsibility to let the world see Jesus through the way you live your life. His Holy Spirit enables you follow Him, and your task is made easier by knowing that Jesus understands because He walked this same path through the world.

JESUS' RESURRECTION IS REAL

"Do not be afraid, for I know that you are looking for Jesus, who was crucified. He is not here; He has risen, just as He said." (Matthew 28:5-6)

Without Jesus' resurrection, Christianity would have been a long-forgotten religion. His principles touch our hearts, stimulate our thoughts, and inspire innumerable charity organizations. Jesus courageously faced death, and conquered it. He rose from the dead and promised to be with His followers forever.

It is the living Christ who reigns in the lives of multitudes of people in the new millennium. They committed themselves to Christ and their worship of Him is a personal choice, not a response to an organization or religious tradition. They meet Him daily in quiet seclusion and are constantly aware of His living presence.

These people may be unable to give a clearly delineated defense of their faith. They probably have little theological training, but deep in their inner being they know that Christ lives, that He loves them and has made them His own.

No one can undermine their faith in the risen and glorified Savior who lives and reigns in their hearts and lives.

THE CHOICE IS YOURS

"What shall I do, then, with Jesus who is called Christ?"
Pilate asked. (Matthew 27:22)

What are we going to do about the polluting of our planet? How are we going to deal with rising costs and devaluation of money? How are we going to channel the energy of the young in the right direction. There are many more similar issues that concern people, but there is one question that is paramount: "What shall I do with Jesus who is called Christ?"

This is not a new problem. Pilate asked the same question 2000 years ago. So much depends on the answer. The wrong answer can mean that you lose everything that is worth anything.

To remain silent is to reject Christ. Some people, like Pilate, theatrically wash their hands announcing that they do not want to have anything to do with Christ. Some people oppose Him. With their lives they shout, "Away with Him! Crucify Him!"

But others, praise the Lord, choose Him as their Redeemer and King. By accepting Christ, they find redemption from sin and death. They gain peace, joy, and eternal life.

Jesus' simple teachings

*Then He told them many things
in parables. (Matthew 13:3)*

One of the marvelous things about Christ is the simplicity of His teachings. He expressed the great truths of His heavenly Father in a way that uneducated people could understand, yet He also confronted the scholars of His time and silenced them with His wisdom. The unique feature of His teachings was their practicality.

He challenged people to forgive their enemies and make friends with them. In His teachings, as well as through His example, He showed the importance of love. The simplicity of faith, as He taught it, leads to a practical, devout lifestyle that transcends theological theories. Everyone who was willing to listen to Him and learn from Him understood what He wanted to tell them.

Remember that the simple elements of Christ's teachings are accessible to everyone, and all can delight in them. To love Him and to love your neighbor through Him; to experience His strength in your spirit; to know that His presence is with you at all times – these are simple yet profound truths that ultimately become a glorious reality in your life.

TRUE CHRISTIANITY

Examine yourselves to see whether you are in the faith; test yourselves. Do you not realize that Christ Jesus is in you? (2 Corinthians 13:5)

Many people think Christians are weak, dull, and ineffective. Christians are often regarded as a species living in a world of their own, removed from the realities of life. They are seen as flocking together to pray and read the Bible while cutting themselves off from the world. Of course, this is a complete misconception of the Christian faith.

There was nothing weak, commonplace, or ineffective about Jesus Christ. The Scriptures bear witness to His humanity and His divinity; to His firmness and His tenderness; to His courage and His humility; and above all, to His love, even when He was subjected to bitter hatred, barbaric torture and death.

Our Leader set this example for all Christians to follow if we wish to be faithful to our highest calling as Christians. This is something that cannot be accomplished in our own strength. That is why God gave us the Holy Spirit.

If you surrender your life to Him completely, He will transform you into a strong and effective witness of the powerful truth of the gospel of Christ.

JESUS GIVES SPIRITUAL WEALTH

And you have been given fullness in Christ, who is the head over every power and authority. (Colossians 2:10)

Through the ages people have gathered goods in order to provide for life today and for the future. This is a good thing and should be encouraged. The danger doesn't lie in the gathering of possessions, but in the obsession to do so. When material goods become overwhelmingly important in your life, you fall prey to the destructiveness of covetousness and desire. Your focus on benefiting yourself means you have little time to consider the needs of others. Worst of all is that your desire to fulfill your responsibilities toward God diminishes.

Christ must be in the center of everything you do. Your complete faith and trust must be in Him at all times. Your persistent prayer must be that you will remain sensitive to the prompting of the Holy Spirit.

If you live such a Christ-centered life, you will find that He meets all your needs. He will inspire you to serve Him among your fellow men. Through His rich grace you will live a life of complete fulfillment. Make sure that you are not so bound to earthly goods that you drift away from Christ.

Are you seeking Jesus?

But Herod said, "I beheaded John. Who, then, is this I hear such things about?" And he tried to see him. (Luke 9:9)

There are many people who seek Jesus in worship, meditation, prayer, and Bible study. They attend silent retreats or go to conferences, seminars, and workshops in an attempt to come face to face with the Son of God. Thousands attend evangelical gatherings in the hope of finding Christ in the ecstasy of worship or in the drama of divine healing and conversions.

There are also those whose faith has lost its fervor, and so they renew their attempts to return to Christ. Many succeed and enjoy renewed communion with the Master. Others fail and their spiritual life remains barren, stark, and desolate; their faith fades and they drift further and further from Him.

If you sincerely and earnestly seek Jesus, there is one certain way of finding Him: seek Him among needy people. He will be with you in any deed of compassion that you perform. The Christ that you seek lives in the hearts and minds of people, and in the smile of gratitude that you receive when you bestow love and compassion on others.

THE FULLNESS OF CHRIST

For God was pleased to have all His fullness dwell in Him, and through Him to reconcile to Himself all things. (Colossians 1:19-20)

According to the Bible, it is not sufficient to maintain that Jesus was simply "a good person". This is because He was more than good: He was the personification of perfection. Paul attempts to define the person of Christ by saying that, "God was pleased to have all His fullness dwell in Him."

This breathtaking truth is so overwhelming that we could hesitate to approach the Lord. But, if He is your Savior, there is no barrier that can separate you from Him. Then John 10:10 becomes true in your life, "I have come that they may have life, and have it to the full." Then life becomes filled with fullness and festivity!

Read Ephesians 3:17-18 again today, "So that Christ may dwell in your hearts through faith. And I pray that you, being rooted and established in love, may have power, together with all the saints, to grasp how wide and long and high and deep is the love of Christ."

How privileged we are, as His children, to partake in this festival of love.

JESUS IS ALIVE TODAY!

"He is not here; He has risen, just as He said." (Matthew 28:6)

On the Sunday morning following the crucifixion, women brought spices to Jesus' tomb. But there was no sign of death there, only of pulsating life. Luke records, "Why do you look for the living among the dead?" (Luke 24:5). Glorious comfort from God to a sorrowful, anxious, and dumbfounded humanity.

He who died for our sins is not dead. He lives! He is in the heaven of His glory where we will live with Him forever. Through His Spirit, He resides in the blessed Gospel that brings hope to our despondent hearts.

Jesus is with us to strengthen, guide, govern, and inspire us to new life. Through His Spirit, He resides in the hearts that He made alive.

The heavenly messenger concluded, "Go quickly and tell His disciples: 'He has risen from the dead ...'" (Matt. 28:7). That is our calling and duty: to spread the word of a living Savior. It is far more fragrant than burial spices. Its aroma should spread through the entire world to give new courage to the brokenhearted and the dying: A fragrance of life to life!

REFLECT CHRIST'S PRESENCE

When Moses came down from Mount Sinai with the two tablets of the Testimony in his hands, he was not aware that his face was radiant because he had spoken with the Lord. (Exodus 34:29)

Often it is possible to tell at a glance what kind of person you are dealing with, which emotions he is experiencing, and whether he is trustworthy. However, we often judge other people wrongly, and so are often disappointed.

You never have to doubt a person who has an intimate relationship with the living Christ. It will always be evident, because the love and compassion of Christ is visible in that person since he looks at you through the eyes of Jesus.

If you cultivate an intimate relationship with Jesus, you will become more and more like Him, because His Holy Spirit is working in you and reaches out to others through you.

Invite Him into your life and allow His love to flow through you to others. Then you will live a life of abundance, which only Jesus can give you (John 10:10).

CHRIST'S INVITATION TO YOU

*"Whoever comes to me I will never
drive away." (John 6:37)*

Many people hesitate to make a full commitment to Jesus Christ. They consider all the things they will have to give up. They know that in their heart they cannot harbor both Christ and sin.

When Jesus Christ says, "Come to Me!", He offers a complete and satisfying life that deals a death blow to sin. It is, therefore, necessary to repent and confess your sins when you respond to His invitation.

Many people find it embarrassing to respond to an emotional evangelical appeal. Their attitude is a barrier of pride that prevents them from experiencing the greatest blessing on earth.

Others, who have disappointed Christ many times, think that if they try to follow Him again, it will make a mockery of His merciful invitation. Regardless of the number of times that you have been unfaithful to the Master, or of the barriers that hold you back, remember that His invitation still stands. He still says, "Come!" and if you respond to Him, He will receive you with open arms.

LET CHRIST LIGHT UP YOUR LIFE

The LORD will be your everlasting light, and your God will be your glory. (Isaiah 60:19)

Perhaps problems are weighing heavily on your mind; perhaps life seems to be empty and meaningless; your dreams may have collapsed like a house of cards: plans may have come to nothing! And so you search for something to lift you out of the quicksand of despair and despondency and add new meaning and purpose to your life.

The solution to your problem lies in accepting Jesus Christ as your personal Savior and Redeemer. Christ came to this world to light up lives that are in darkness. He brought healing for the body and for the spirit. Those who have been touched by Him have found their lives transformed by His divine presence.

If the light has gone out in your life and you are stumbling in the dark, seek the living Christ in prayer and meditation, in His eternal Word, in the beauty of creation, and in the quietness of your room.

Gradually His power will flow into your life. His light will light up the shadows in your life, and His peace will flood your heart with serenity.

WHEN JESUS ENTERS YOUR LIFE

"Blessed is the king who comes in the name of the Lord! Peace in heaven and glory in the highest!" (Luke 19:38)

When we read about Jesus' triumphant journey into Jerusalem, we sense the joy and excitement of those who welcomed Him so enthusiastically. He was the long-awaited Messiah who would usher in an era of peace, joy, hope, and liberation.

People throughout the ages who have welcomed Christ into their lives, have experienced similar joy. Jesus came so that you can experience the fullness of life (John 10:10). This means that you can live in peace, assured that He is with you at all times.

Just as the people of Jerusalem were under the yoke of the Roman oppressors, so today many people are enslaved by detrimental habits. The living Christ offers to liberate you from these habits. Others are seeking love, mercy, and compassion in a world that, at times, seems very cruel. Jesus still offers this to those who accept Him as their Redeemer and Savior today.

When you welcome the Master into your life with the same excitement felt by the people of Jerusalem, Christ's joy and peace will fill your life.

GROW IN CHRIST

Paul says that Jesus Christ and the eternal God are equal, and declares, with great boldness, that the One is like the Other. You may be overwhelmed by the fact that you can see the person of God in the living Christ.

This truth stirs your soul, and you may feel that such spiritual heights are beyond your reach. Jesus lived on such a high moral level, setting examples of how to respond in certain situations and you realize that you cannot live up to His example on your own.

On the other hand, this great truth also inspires and elevates us. The living Christ does not condemn people for their sins, but inspires them to reach unprecedented heights. The eternal God presented Jesus Christ as an example to us of what we must aspire to. Depending on the strength and intensity of our devotion to Him, we can, in a small way, become like Jesus.

That is God's purpose for your life. As you attempt to reach this objective, you will find that you are walking the path of fulfillment, peace, and happiness.

CHRIST'S MINISTRY PURPOSE

God ... gave us the ministry of reconciliation:
that God was reconciling the world to Himself
in Christ, not counting men's sins against
them. (2 Corinthians 5:18-19)

The great separation between God and humankind took place when man, in disobedience, declared himself to be independent of God. He thought that this would liberate him, but in reality he became the slave of influences stronger than himself. The egotistical *I* replaced God; love turned into sensuality. Man's declaration of independence from God was disastrous. Subsequent events proved that humankind cannot rule the world in their own wisdom and strength.

Even though humanity turned away from God, God did not turn away from His people. The purpose of Christ's coming into this world as a man was to bridge the gaping chasm that separated man from God.

Through Christ's ministry God revealed to us what we can become through His strength. We can be liberated from sin, share in the enriching experience of His Spirit living in us, and experience ongoing communion with Him.

God has not changed. His love is eternal and those who accept Christ and follow His ways find their relationship with God is fully restored.

CHRIST LIVES!

But Christ has indeed been raised from the dead, the firstfruits of those who have fallen asleep. (1 Corinthians 15:20)

It is a glorious truth that Jesus Christ conquered death and that He is triumphantly alive today, just as He was alive when He appeared to His disciples after His death on the cross.

His resurrection revealed a new dimension of the power of God. To believe that Christ lives, that He lives today, and to order your life according to this overwhelming fact, are the deepest roots of the true Christian experience.

Although Christ is alive and still present with us, He can only work in the lives of those who acknowledge Him as their Master, Lord, and Guide. Although He is with you always, there are times when you are not completely "with Him."

Often your thoughts and deeds seem to contradict the truth of His presence. If you were able to see Him face to face, you would not even consider doing half the things you do in His invisible presence!

How you respond to the truth that Christ lives, is proof of the sincerity and the quality of your faith.

THE RESURRECTION MEANS ...

"Why do you look for the living among the dead?" (Luke 24:5)

Luther said, "Even if Christ was born a thousand times in Bethlehem and not yet in your heart, you will still be lost." In the same vein we can declare, "Even though Christ rose miraculously from the dead but has not risen in your heart, you will still be lost."

- Christ's resurrection expels all doubt. Like Thomas' doubt, mine must turn into worshiping assurance, "My Lord and my God."
- The resurrection expels all fear. I no longer fear the enemies of the cross; neither sin, nor Satan, nor death. Christ triumphed over them all.
- The resurrection expels loneliness. The lonely of this world can rejoice, because the resurrected Savior said, "And surely I am with you always" (Matt. 28:20).
- The resurrection expels my fear of death. Paul assures us that, "Death has been swallowed up in victory" (1 Cor. 15:54).
- The resurrection gives me a testimony. The church lives and grows because of those who testify that they have a message from a living and redeeming Christ who has risen from the dead!

CLOSE TO GOD THROUGH CHRIST

You who once were far away have been brought near through the blood of Christ. (Ephesians 2:13)

We joyously commemorate the coming of Christ into this world as one of us. Christ, the Light of the World, became flesh, but was without sin. When the word *flesh* is used to describe us, it carries in it the sense of our blemished nature, for Christ alone was flesh without sin.

The Word – and our experience – testifies to the fact that our flesh is in a constant battle with the Spirit. Paul says in Romans 8:7 that the mind set on the flesh is hostile to God.

But Christ was not marred by sin. He became our equal in everything except in sin. This is the glorious message of the Gospel: Emmanuel! God with us! Jesus Christ, Son of God, descended from heaven to prepare the way for humankind to be restored to the Father's favor. He came to redeem a lost world.

First there was God above, God far from us; then, in Christ, God was with us; and now, through the Holy Spirit, God is in us.

APRIL

SALVATION AND REDEMPTION

Broken, cleansed and useful

And I said, "Here am I. Send me!" (Isaiah 6:8)

It is important to know what God expects you to do for Him, but there is another question we must consider before we serve Him, "Lord, what must I *be*?"

I must be saved. Isaiah was a prophet of the Lord, yet his life changed radically when he met God. Shattered with guilt, he fell at the feet of his Lord, and cried, "Woe to me! I am ruined!"

Nicodemus was a religious man, but Christ cut to the core his relationship with God: "You must be born again."

God cleanses us from sin. A glowing coal from the altar must touch my life. I must be purified of selfishness, wrong attitudes, spiritual bankruptcy, and every wickedness of my heart. The Holy Spirit must purify my thinking, my life, and my actions.

Only then can the Lord use me. Then I will answer cheerfully, "Here I am, Lord! Send me!" Then I will do His work faithfully, since I believe in the power of prayer; in the sanctifying work of the Holy Spirit; in the preciousness of souls; in the Word of God.

The cross
in the Middle

When they came to the place called the Skull, there they
crucified Him, along with the criminals – one on
His right, the other on His left. (Luke 23:33)

Golgotha, the smallest hill in Jerusalem, seldom finds a place in a list of the mighty mountains that surround the city of David. But for us Golgotha is the grandest, most precious, most meaningful of all the majestic mountains on the face of the earth.

Three similar crosses stand there, but they differ from each other as the dark night from the bright day. The central cross is the focal point of the universe because of the Man hanging there. He is holy and righteous, yet in Him, the guilt of all humankind is nailed to the cross. Pilate testifies that he finds no guilt in Him; a Roman officer says, "Surely this was a righteous man" (Luke 23:47).

It is our cross that He hangs on. He bears our guilt, sin, and punishment on that cross of redemption. Jesus died on your cross and exonerated you. We were redeemed from the guilt of all our sin forever and ever. There we receive salvation, forgiveness, and redemption. Let us kneel at the cross, the gate of our city of refuge which is eternal life!

THE JOY OF LIFE IN CHRIST

"Blessed rather are those who hear the word of God and obey it." (Luke 11:28)

Many people regard the observing of religious principles as a tiresome yet necessary discipline because it places restrictions on their pleasure, yet they realize it is important for the well-being of their soul.

Christians should have a more positive attitude to their faith because Jesus came so that you can have life in all its abundance. He wants your life to be filled with purpose, vitality, and joy.

The basis of our Christian experience is a relationship with our caring heavenly Father who wants only the best for His children. He sacrificed His Son on the cross because of His incomprehensibly great love for you. Jesus offers you forgiveness, redemption, and the hope of eternal life. His Holy Spirit enables you to live in trust, confidence, and victory.

What more could anyone ask of life? Here you have the promise of the very best that life can offer, and all that God expects of you is to yield to His sovereignty in your life. This is little enough to ask in exchange for a life of fulfillment and joy.

SPIRITUAL FITNESS

*If we claim to be without sin, we deceive ourselves
and the truth is not in us. (1 John 1:8)*

It is impossible to build a healthy spiritual life on the foundations of a faith that is deteriorating because of stubbornness and deliberate disobedience to God. Spiritual weakness is often the result of our unwillingness to discard things that harm our relationship with God.

Spiritual fitness begins when you open your life to the influence of God's Holy Spirit. This can be a humbling and sometimes even painful experience. When the Spirit draws your attention to cherished sins that are festering in your spirit and blocking your spiritual growth, you need to confess them to your heavenly Father.

God requires a deliberate and specific act of confession from you, because this helps you to be delivered from the destructive influences that have tortured you for so long. Confessing the sins that you would rather forget is the first step on the path of spiritual healing.

When you place the past in God's care and ask for His mercy, you enter a new phase of life and you can meet the future with joy and confidence.

BLOOD IS LIFE!

But if we walk in the light, as He is in the light, we have
fellowship with one another, and the blood of Jesus,
His Son, purifies us from all sin. (1 John 1:7)

When Napoleon was in exile on Saint Helena, he occasionally stood in front of a map on which England was marked in red. He would resentfully point his finger to the red spot and say, "If it were not for that red blotch, I would have conquered the world."

Likewise, Satan probably points to Golgotha and the blood that flowed there, and peevishly says, "If it were not for Golgotha and the blood of the Lamb, I would have conquered the world."

Easter confronts us with the meaning of the blood that flowed on Golgotha. The blood from the cross is the surety that Christ has paid the price for our sins in full. The Lamb was slaughtered and the angel of death passed by.

Jesus, as the true God and as a righteous Man completely free of sin, had to die. Only the blood of Jesus is able to purify us. No sin is too big or too small to be covered by His blood. May you again experience the purification that comes from accepting the sacrifice Christ made for you.

CHRIST'S GIFT TO YOU

But now a righteousness from God, apart from law, has been made known ... This righteousness from God comes through faith in Jesus Christ to all who believe. (Romans 3:21-22)

Many people deny themselves the joy of a life fulfilled in Christ because they are convinced they are not worthy of it. Because of something they have said or done in the past, they believe that they cannot turn to Christ for help. And so they fail to experience Christ's greatest gift to humanity: God's love.

The greatest wonder of the Christian faith is that God has chosen you as His own. Nothing except for the fact that you believe in Jesus Christ qualified you for this privilege. His love cannot be earned and nothing that you do can make you worthy of it. It is God's gift to you, given in abundant grace.

If you find it difficult to accept this fact of salvation, just think of the crucifixion of our Savior. A thief, who lived a life of lawlessness and sin, was crucified with Jesus, and at the very last moment he turned to Jesus for mercy. And Jesus accepted him into Paradise that very day. Regardless of who you are or what your past involves, the love of the living Christ is God's gift to you.

A CHOICE FOR ETERNITY

"What shall I do, then, with Jesus who is called Christ?" (Matthew 27:22)

What must I do with Jesus? My answer to this question will determine where I will spend eternity.

I could *oppose* Him, crying out with the crowds, "Crucify Him! Crucify Him!" Every day we hear people loudly deny the existence of God; they mock the Man of Sorrows. They kneel at the altars of power, position, and materialism. They foolishly believe that they can live without God.

I can also *ignore* Him. Faith is beneath people who ignore Jesus, and they take no notice of Him. They merely tolerate Christianity as they would a winter cold. They are neither warm nor cold; neither for Him nor against Him. However, you cannot wash your hands of Jesus and His suffering. By refusing to choose, you have already chosen against Him.

I can *embrace* Him irrevocably as my Savior and Redeemer, "To all who received Him, to those who believed in His name, He gave the right to become children of God" (John 1:12). I can accept His love, His peace, His salvation. If you embrace Him, you will be able to rejoice today.

GABBATHA: WHAT IS TRUTH?

"What is truth?" Pilate asked. (John 18:38)

There are a few fundamental truths that we, as Christ's disciples, can convey to a world in search of truth:

- All people are guilty before God. It is extremely difficult for man to say: I am a guilty sinner! People try to conceal their sins, to deny them, or to shift the blame. However, the wages of sin is death. And that is the truth.
- Jesus Christ came to this world to deliver us from sin (John 3:16). This is a truth that carries a terrible price – a price that was paid on the cross.
- Each person must discover this glorious truth for himself and then, in response to the Holy Spirit working in his heart, turn to God in sincere repentance for his sins. The cross reminds us anew of this truth: there is still time to discover the truth and respond to it. The Lord is compassionate and gracious, slow to anger, abounding in love.

CRUCIFIED WITH JESUS

They crucified Him, along with the criminals – one on His right, the other on His left. (Luke 23:33)

To the left of Jesus is a cross of rebellion and revolt. A robber, a rebel, and a murderer hangs here. But this is not the worst that can be said about him. He experiences no remorse, even though the Savior of sinners hangs beside him. He hangs next to the almighty Savior, and yet he dies unsaved.

Pay heed to this terrible lesson: someone can live in close proximity to the Savior and still go unsaved. The river of grace can flow right past you but you can die of thirst if you refuse to drink the water of life.

To the right of Jesus, there is a cross of guilt and of repentance. Another villain, no better than the first hangs here. His pitiless life will soon end as well, but he gains eternal life.

This criminal cast himself upon the mercy and love of Jesus. He acknowledges Jesus and confesses his guilt. And Jesus awaits him at the gates of eternity and guides him, the very first fruit of the cross, into heaven. The angels rejoice over this one sinner who has been redeemed.

WHY GOLGOTHA?

"My God, my God, why have You forsaken me?" (Matthew 27:46)

Why do bad things happen to good people? Why is there war, terrorism, murder, and hatred? Does God know about it – and does He care? Yes, a thousand times yes! That is why there was a cross on Golgotha where His own Son cried, "My God, my God, why have You forsaken me?"

Why did Jesus have to die on a cursed tree?

- The wrath of God demanded it. Man, created in the image of God, fell in sin and the death penalty was handed down: the wages of sin is death.
- The love of God required it. The sins of humanity had to be paid for. The love of God found an answer in the sacrifice of His Son.
- Christ chose for it to be so. Christ's obedience to the Father caused Him to become a man and die on the cross at Golgotha.

Christ did it to redeem us. Golgotha teaches us that God's love is unfathomable and, as we appropriate it for ourselves, we gain eternal life.

JESUS UNDERSTANDS

Jesus wept. Then the Jews said, "See how He loved him!" (John 11:35-36)

There are people who are skeptical of any suggestion that Jesus understands human problems. They see Him as Someone aloof and far removed from our everyday life, concerned only with matters of universal importance. They think He cannot be concerned with the inconsequential details of their personal lives.

This is a complete misconception of God and His loving interest in the world that He created and the human beings for whom His Son died and was resurrected.

Never lose sight of the fact that Jesus is not only your Master, but also your Friend. Because He lived, suffered, and died as a human being, He understands human problems and emotions. He endured suffering, as well as disappointment, sorrow, and joy. The Son of God laughed and cried just as you and I do.

The Savior is waiting for you to invite Him to share your life with Him. Open your heart to Him so that He can help you in whatever circumstances you may find yourself. Never forget that He is a friend who loves you and understands you.

LIFE PARTNERS

"I no longer call you servants, because a servant does not know his master's business. Instead, I have called you friends, for everything that I learned from My Father I have made known to you." (John 15:15)

It is only when you have sincerely asked the risen Christ to become your life partner that you begin to understand the full impact and implications of your Christian faith. When Christ is in control, your life is completely transformed.

The purpose of the ministry of Christ is to reconcile you with the Father. Your part is to acknowledge His sovereignty and His redemptive power in your life. Then you will be more and more aware of His presence in your daily life, because you are following the path that Christ has mapped out for you.

To live your life in partnership with God and with a focus on spiritual matters, brings your life into perfect balance. When Christ is in control of your life, your behavior in all things is inspired by the Holy Spirit and He wants the best for you.

You will not be a silent partner, but will eagerly demonstrate your role in this partnership in every aspect of your life. And others will see your life filled with the abundance of God's grace.

SALVATION: FACT, NOT FICTION

"Everyone who calls on the name of the Lord will be saved." (Romans 10:13)

The Word of God has pride of place as the most widely read book of all times. The faith that is ignited and inspired by the Word can never be equaled by anything the world offers. In its pages we find the Treasure of the Ages.

Regardless of who you are: saint or hardened sinner; regardless of what you may do: good or evil; the living Christ offers you salvation and eternal life in God's eternal kingdom. All that is required of you is to turn to God in repentance, confess your sins, and embrace Him as your Savior and Redeemer.

For many, the gospel message appears too simple to be true. They allow their cynicism to rob them of the greatest source of peace at man's disposal. Look around you and see how Christ has changed people's lives: they did not buy or work for their salvation. They received it freely through repentance and confession: "Salvation is found in no one else, for there is no other name under heaven given to men by which we must be saved" (Acts 4:12).

SIN WILL COST YOU DEARLY

The soul who sins is the one who will die. (Ezekiel 18:4)

In modern society sin has lost its sting. It has been diluted with psychological terms and referred to as weaknesses or illnesses. But the consequences of sin still remain the same. Sin separates us from God, creates feelings of guilt, inferiority, and frustration, and robs sinners of peace of mind.

Your sin will eventually find you out. Many people try to ignore this fact with all their might. They believe that they are the exception to the divine law that says we reap what we sow.

People give no thought to the consequences of sin. Sin can be extremely costly; we cannot calculate how much sadness and sorrow is inflicted upon the world because of sin.

When you sin, you isolate yourself from God by following your own path and deviating from God's way. To accept Jesus Christ as your personal Redeemer and Savior, and to consciously live in the presence of God, is the only way to preserve yourself from sin. In this way you will experience freedom and be set free from your guilt as the Holy Spirit enables you to live victoriously.

MISSION ACCOMPLISHED

When He had received the drink, Jesus said,
"It is finished." (John 19:30)

The Greek word *Tetelestai* is the victorious cry of the Victor, Jesus. What was finished that gave rise to this victorious cry?

- The Old Testament prophecies were fulfilled. Jesus Christ was born in Bethlehem and was counted among the poor. His body was pierced, His clothes divided, His dignity mocked.
- Victory over the enemy was complete. Darkness was overcome by brilliant light. Satan's power was broken and destroyed. Christ went to prepare a place for us and will once again return in glory to take us to be where He is.
- Man's salvation is complete. The demands of God's righteousness were met. He redeemed us with His blood. Our debt has been paid, the warrant for our arrest nailed to the cross. Sin no longer rules us. Jesus triumphed, conquering Satan, sin, death, and hell. It is finished!

How can we escape if we trample such great salvation under our feet?

THE CAUSE OF HIS SUFFERING

But He was pierced for our transgressions, He was crushed for our iniquities; the punishment that brought us peace was upon Him, and by His wounds we are healed. (Isaiah 53:5)

Jesus took the sins of the world upon Himself and bore them vicariously for our atonement. God took our unrighteousness upon Him and He was punished for our transgressions. Jesus suffered all through His life, from the crib to the cross, "Look around and see. Is any suffering like My suffering that was inflicted on Me?" (Lam. 1:12).

God's wrath is the all-consuming fire of His holiness that works to destroy sin. Some people do not want to hear anything about God's wrath. God is love, they say. We agree with this fully. But God is also holy and we dare not consider His holiness as less important than His love. Wrath is at its most severe when it is justly conveyed by love. God is just in His love. Therefore, He could not let sin go unpunished.

And that is why I implore you, look at Christ in His incomparable sorrow, brought upon Him by a just God in His wrath. Our God, who is endlessly just, is also endlessly great in love and grace. That is our hope and our salvation.

THE NEVER-ENDING QUEST

"If only I knew where to find Him; if only I could go to His dwelling!" (Job 23:3)

Humankind's innate yearning for God is revealed in a multitude of ways. The first indication of spiritual hunger is a restlessness that cannot be appeased. One of the encouraging facts about our spiritual hunger that is often overlooked is that God is always waiting to satisfy every person's spiritual hunger. It is not the Father's will for any of His children to drift from the sphere of His love and become unhappy with their lives.

The message of the gospel is that our heavenly Father is waiting to receive every one of His children into a full and enriching relationship with Himself. This is His fervent desire for all people, and is the reason why He sent Jesus Christ to earth.

In order to experience this profound intimacy, it is essential to turn away from your stubborn disobedience to God and in faith to accept the gift of Jesus' salvation. Allow God's Spirit to fill your life so that Jesus can live in you. It is the only way for your hunger for God to be satisfied.

THE UNAVOIDABLE QUESTION

"What shall I do, then, with Jesus who is called Christ?" (Matthew 27:22)

The cardinal question of life is the Pilate question: "What shall I do with Jesus who is called Christ?" The right answer can mean that you win everything for time and eternity – the wrong answer could mean that you will lose everything.

There are those who prefer ignoring Jesus. Like Pilate they ostentatiously wash their hands and then announce theatrically that they have nothing to do with the entire business. However, it is not that easy to ignore Him. Your destiny is inextricably bound to Jesus Christ.

There are people who choose to oppose Christ. They shout themselves hoarse, "Away with Him. Crucify Him!" They want to shout Christ out of their lives. It is futile and self-destructive and can end only in inglorious defeat.

There are those who accept Him. They accept Him as Redeemer and Savior. He rules their lives. Set free from sin and condemnation, they obtain peace of mind, joy, righteousness and eternal life.

Life without Christ is a hopeless end; life with Christ is an endless hope.

THE WAY OUT OF MY DISTRESS

Then I acknowledged my sin to You and did not cover up my iniquity. I said, "I will confess my transgressions to the Lord" – and You forgave the guilt of my sin. (Psalm 32:5)

We are living in a world broken and torn apart by sin. Countless dangers surround us, many sinister temptations assault us, many enslaving ties bind us. We are forced into the prison of despair and sit trapped within the cold walls in which sin has imprisoned us.

There is a way out of this misery. Jesus Christ holds the key. It begins when we confess our sins in sincere repentance as David did of old – as the lost son did when he returned from a distant country to his father's house and heart, and life became a celebration of his freedom.

When you come to Christ with your messed-up life and confess your sins, forget the failures and disappointments of the past and reach out for the new life in Him. Forget your disgrace and shame and accept that you are a child of God. Forget your defeats and follow Christ on the road of victory.

God is merciful and strong and if you fight sin in His powerful name you will walk with confidence and a song of deliverance in your heart and on your lips.

He knows and understands

*He did not need man's testimony about man,
for He knew what was in a man. (John 2:25)*

Just because Christ understands your weaknesses does not mean that He condones your sins. He, who was tempted like us in all respects, has called you to a life of victory through the power of His Holy Spirit. Unfortunately, those things that people like to gloss over by calling them *weaknesses*, and which are really just sins, rob our spiritual life of its vitality.

As far as Christ is concerned there are no insignificant sins, because all sin separates us from the Lord. Christ understands human weakness and frailty, offers forgiveness, purifies us, saves us, and gives us the spiritual strength to live victoriously.

Christ looks beyond our sin and sees what we can become through the power of the Holy Spirit. He does not see us as struggling, failed, and imperfect beings, but as channels of the grace of God, doing His will in the sphere of life where He has placed us. Because He knows what people are like, He knows our potential and desires to lead us to the perfection that God has ordained for us.

Blessings for
a broken heart

*Speak tenderly to Jerusalem, and proclaim to her that
her hard service has been completed, that her sin has
been paid for, that she has received from the LORD's
hand double for all her sins. (Isaiah 40:2)*

Sorrow for our sins results from many things: apprehension about our betrayal of the living God; awareness of our shallowness, disobedience, and unwillingness to serve Him; sorrow for our lack of holiness
and our refusal to submit to His holy will; uneasiness
at our devotedness to our worldly possessions, and
much more.

However, Jesus, our Savior, comforts all who have
learned, through grace, to grieve over their sins and
who know that, through repentance and forgiveness,
they now belong to Him. At the bitter fountain of
Marah, God showed Moses a piece of wood that made
the bitter water sweet. That piece of wood symbol-
izes the cross to us: through the bitter, cursed tree we
find healing for the source of our sin and sorrow. The
cross becomes a "miracle tree" from which we receive
eternal Comfort in life and in death.

On this tree Christ carried our sins in His body. On
this tree He is fully our Comforter, Savior, and Redeemer.

YOUR CONSCIENCE SPEAKS

"I heard You in the garden, and I was afraid because I was naked; so I hid." (Genesis 3:10)

There are times in our lives when we are bowed down under the burden of guilt, and our consciences condemn us. Some of the innumerable causes of this are those deeds involving half-truths, deception, jealousy, and falsehoods, to name but a few. Some of these appear very insignificant, and yet the human conscience reminds the wrongdoer of his transgression in no uncertain terms.

Because of the feelings of guilt and shame, many people try to conceal their mistakes by trying to shut them out of their thoughts. Others try to justify their behavior. They think this will help to calm the storm that is so often the result of sin.

One thing is absolutely certain: however hard you try, you cannot hide your transgressions from God. Regardless of the steps you take to conceal the offence, the radiant light of Jesus Christ will reveal it before your all-knowing Father.

Never try to hide from God. Remember His love, and confess the things that you are ashamed of to Him. Then gratefully receive His forgiveness and the peace that is the result of true repentance.

The promise of a new life

A shoot will come up from the stump of Jesse; from his roots a Branch will bear fruit. (Isaiah 11:1)

Centuries ago, the royal house of David stood at the center of the nation like a tall and majestic tree. But over time it was chopped down. The glory of the house of David waned. And yet, through God's omnipotence and mercy, a shoot came up from the meager remnant of the once powerful house of David. The shoot that Isaiah prophesies of is none other than Jesus Christ.

This humble shoot grew up into a mighty tree, which spread its branches to the ends of the earth. The Child in the manger grew up to become the way, the truth, and the life. He wields God's scepter of righteousness over the whole earth and His reign knows no end.

As we contemplate this, we must first humbly assess our own spiritual decay and confess our sins before the Lord. From the stump of Jesse He brought forth new life, a new dispensation, a new period of spiritual growth for those who had fallen away: "He who was seated on the throne said, 'I am making everything new!'" (Rev. 21:5). And that includes you.

THE EXTENT OF CHRIST'S LOVE

Do you show contempt for the riches of His kindness, tolerance and patience, not realizing that God's kindness leads you toward repentance? (Romans 2:4)

It is only when you take note of all the evil in the world and take into consideration the untrustworthiness of people, that you become aware of the full extent of God's love. People ignore Him, they forget the manifestations of His grace, they disobey Him, rebel against Him, and blame Him when things go wrong in their lives. And still, in His love, God sent Christ to live among us and to die for us so that we could find salvation and eternal life.

No human being would have tolerated the attitude that humankind displays toward God, and then still persevere in infinite love as God does towards His people. That is what one starts to appreciate as the true meaning of the Christian faith. Christianity is rooted in the great love of God that transcends our understanding.

Acknowledge His gracious acceptance of you as His child. Surrender yourself unconditionally to His Son. Follow Him and live life to the full as He offers it to you (John 10:10).

Praise the Lord, because He is good. His love is infinite.

RECEIVE GOD'S FORGIVENESS

I prayed to the Lord my God and confessed. (Daniel 9:4)

One of the great privileges and joys of the Christian faith is that no matter what you have done, God is always waiting for you to turn to Him in prayer. His love for you is so vast that you are assured of His forgiveness even before you enter into His presence. All that you have to do is turn in repentance to Christ and confess all your sins to Him.

Maybe it is precisely because it seems so simple and easy that so many people do not accept this glorious gift of grace from Christ. Or maybe they are too ashamed to confess their failures.

There are two important matters that you need to consider. One is that God knows everything about you, including your weaknesses and shortcomings. The other is that despite it all He still loves you and always will. He proved it when Christ died on the cross for you.

Open your heart to Him and lay your guilt and fear before His throne of grace. Here you will experience the purifying balm of His unfathomable love.

PRAYER FOR FORGIVENESS

"Father, forgive them, for they do not know what they are doing." (Luke 23:34)

In the moment of deepest sorrow, Christ utters a prayer; not for revenge, but one of compassion and redemption. In the midst of such great suffering He knew that He had a loving Father. That was His anchor of peace in the midst of the storm. He is our Father too and in our deepest sorrow we too can pray to Him. He understands because His Son's sorrow was also His sorrow.

It is also a prayer of compassion and understanding, "They do not know what they are doing." Jesus prays for others, not for Himself. He pardons, rather than condemns them. He does not want to destroy; He wants to redeem.

During His ministry on earth, He preached love: here He demonstrates it. And He expects every disciple of His to do the same.

Jesus knows that the sinner's salvation lies in the forgiveness of God. Until the very end He loved and forgave.

He is still interceding for us. He does not desire revenge and our death. He wants to pardon our sins so that we can live.

SHARE IN THE LIFE OF CHRIST

God, who has called you into fellowship with His Son Jesus Christ our Lord, is faithful. (1 Corinthians 1:9)

To share in the life of Christ opens up immense possibilities for us, but also huge responsibilities. Your understanding of God deepens, your vision of what your life could be broadens, and you become aware of the constant presence of Christ in your life.

Such an intimacy with the Master brings with it definite responsibilities. Your life must reflect what you believe. The holy characteristics of God must be evident in your daily life through love, integrity, selflessness, and the purity of your goals.

As you, to the best of your ability, display the nature of Christ in your life, the vision of what you can do for the Lord begins to crystallize. You will no longer be restricted by secret fears and doubts, but will face the future with faith in the power of the living Christ.

Christ gave Himself for you so that you can share your life with Him. You might be aware of this glorious truth, but until you claim it as your own through faith, you will not experience the joy and strength of Christ in your spiritual life.

OUR SOURCE
OF HAPPINESS

*"Hosanna! Blessed is He who comes in the name
of the Lord! Blessed is the coming kingdom of
our father David!" (Mark 11:9-10)*

To be blessed, we must know Jesus as our personal
Savior and Redeemer; we must commit our lives to
Him; we must be obedient to His will.

Our expectations regarding blessing, and God's
way of providing it, often differ widely. Through
the ages, this has presented many problems: Adam
and Eve, the people of Israel, and even the disciples
searched for a worldly kingdom, while Christ came
to build a heavenly one.

We search for happiness but we want it on our
terms and so we run the risk of missing Christ's blessing. Human happiness often depends upon chance or
luck: a sudden change in our condition. One moment
we have nothing, and then, suddenly, we have wealth
and abundance. Human happiness is something that
life offers, and then, just as suddenly, rips away. Man,
in his short-sightedness, calls it "happiness" when
things go his way for a while.

But God's view on happiness and blessing is vastly
different. Christ's happiness is a happiness that is
different, a joy in Him.

AWAKE MY SOUL!

"Our friend Lazarus has fallen asleep: but I am going there to wake him up." (John 11:11)

How appropriate Jesus' words are for us today! There are many people who need to be woken from their indifference, their hopelessness, and their helplessness. They nurture the worries and anxieties that torture them daily. They forget that, in the midst of all the problems in the world today, it is not only important, but imperative, that your whole life should be grounded on your faith in the living Christ. This is your guarantee of a new life of powerful faith.

It is easy to give in to the temptation, just to give up the fight and drift along with the current rather than living the life God expects you to. If you are trusting in your own resources and ingenuity, there is little doubt that you will go under.

Nevertheless, just as Christ raised Lazarus from the dead, He will raise you from your spiritual stupor and inspire you to live a life of victory and success in His service. The only thing that the life-giving Savior asks of you is that you accept Him as the Lord of your life. Can you afford to refuse an offer so rich in mercy?

LIFE IN ALL ITS FULLNESS

*That you may be filled to the measure of all
the fullness of God. (Ephesians 3:19)*

There are people who, because of circumstances or negative dispositions, have descended into a mire of despair. They have lost interest in life and in the fullness that life has to offer.

While we will experience setbacks in life, which at times rock the foundations of our very existence, we must never lose sight of the Jesus factor. He came so that we may have abundant life (John 10:10). He assures us that, in every situation, He will be with us (Matt. 28:20), He promised that He would carry our burden with us (Matt. 11:28-30). All that we need to do is turn to Him in faith.

If you are depressed, you need to enter into an intimate relationship with the living Christ through prayer and meditation. Tell Him all your problems and concerns. Share your doubts and your fears with Him. Do that and you will experience profound joy and peace.

Through God's immense grace you will find meaning and direction for your life, and your life will be crowned with the success of God.

MAY

THE HOLY SPIRIT

POWER FROM ON HIGH

*"But you will receive power when the
Holy Spirit comes on you." (Acts 1:8)*

There are many well-meaning Christians who never
succeed in developing their full potential because
they don't understand the person and work of the
Holy Spirit. This has a negative influence on their
discipleship, and they are unable to serve Christ as
effectively as they should.

If you depend on your own strength in your service to the Master, you are sure to fail. Jesus Himself
said, " ... apart from Me you can do nothing" (John
15:5).

This is not something that you can earn or make
happen through your own effort. The anointing is the
gift of grace you receive when you submit yourself
to the authority of the living Christ, and when you
diligently seek Him in prayer and willingly receive
the blessing and the privilege and the responsibility
of this gift.

Accept God's gift with gratitude and joy, and allow the Spirit to lead you along the ways of service
that He has ordained for you. Then serve Him with a
new-found spirit of trust, authority, and peace.

CHRISTIAN GROWTH

"Remain in Me, and I will remain in you." (John 15:4)

Perhaps your spiritual life has lost some of its fervor. If so, it is time that you pause for a while and prayerfully seek the reason for this.

You might have drifted away from Christ. You may be focusing on something that is good in itself, but is ultimately inadequate to satisfy your deepest longing and needs.

Faith founded on Jesus is alive and vibrant. Jesus regards His relationship with you and your relationship with Him as extremely important. And the miracle of His grace is that He gives His Holy Spirit to us to fill our lives so that He can manifest Himself through us. If we place Him first, all other things will fall into their proper perspective.

There are some misinformed people who think that such commitment to Christ will rob life of its vitality and excitement. They, unfortunately, have only a vague understanding of the Lord. He has come to give life – life that is abundant and rich. This is the inheritance of those in whom He lives, and who abide in Him.

LIFE IN THE SPIRIT

We know that we live in Him and He in us, because He has given us of His Spirit. (1 John 4:13)

The wonder of God's grace is that Christ can live in you. Scripture clearly proclaims, "This is how you can recognize the Spirit of God: Every spirit that acknowledges that Jesus Christ has come in the flesh is from God" (1 John 4:2-3).

The basic prerequisite for a true Christian life is to unconditionally surrender your life to Christ. When His Spirit fills our hearts and lives, we find new meaning in life. And this causes our hearts to overflow with joy and peace beyond measure.

When you fully accept God's Spirit into your life, a miracle takes place. This is the first step in Christian discipleship. But there must be continual and consistent growth. You have to develop a deeper understanding of God so that you can faithfully obey His will.

When you allow the Spirit of God into your life, He begins to transform you so that you no longer live to satisfy your own desires, but to do the will of God whom you love. Don't hesitate to walk in the Spirit. It is the only way to find fulfillment, joy, and peace!

THE HOLY SPIRIT'S STRENGTH

I pray that out of His glorious riches He may strengthen you with power through His Spirit. (Ephesians 3:16)

Much has been said about the necessity of putting Christ first in your life and submitting yourself to His will and obeying His commandments. Christians are urged to turn away from the demands of this world and joyfully follow Christ. Countless sincere believers have tried to measure up to these demands but often find that it is much easier said than done.

It requires a measure of willpower and a strength of character that are far beyond the capacity of the average person to live a life that fulfills the requirements of Jesus Christ.

The stress of modern life places us under enormous pressure, which increases when we need to testify for Him in circumstances that directly contradict a Christian lifestyle.

It is precisely in these circumstances that you need to open your life to the Holy Spirit. Invite Him to take control of your entire life and you will experience the power of Jesus that enables you to overcome all obstacles while enabling you to live for, through, and in Him.

TOGETHER WITH GOD

*I can do everything through him who
gives me strength. (Philippians 4:13)*

The Holy Spirit of God, who fills God's entire creation, can also live in your heart. Accepting this truth releases the power of God in your life.

When you think of yourself as a part of God's revelation of Himself, you enter an intimacy with Him that will bring strength, balance, and vitality into your life. But it also engenders a strong sense of responsibility in you. When you realize that God created you and that you are governed by His Spirit, you realize that your life should live up to His expectations.

You no longer live to please yourself, but live to do His will. Through the grace of God and His Spirit you live a life pleasing to Him in the strength of the Lord Jesus Christ.

Before our Savior ascended to heaven He promised that His Spirit would come to those who accept Him as Savior and Lord. It is the Holy Spirit who makes God a reality in the life of the Christian and who enables us to live in harmony with God.

THE HOLY SPIRIT'S POWER

So I say, live by the Spirit, and you will not gratify the desires of the sinful nature. (Galatians 5:16)

Commitment and surrender to Jesus Christ, obedience to the will of God, and following the example and teachings of Christ, require a high level of dedication and self-discipline, far above normal human ability. That is why many who want to become disciples do not accept the challenge. They too readily succumb to the temptations and seductions of the world.

To enable you to live up to the requirements and challenges of your commitment to Him, Jesus has made His Holy Spirit available to you. He enables you to live as Jesus expects you to live and to overcome the temptations of the world.

If you dedicate yourself to the Lord and allow His Holy Spirit in you to guide you, you will experience the power of the Holy Spirit more and more in your life.

Always remain sensitive to His influence and you will receive power that will enable you to live in obedience to the will of God.

EFFECTIVE CHRISTIANITY

We have been released from the law so that we serve in the new way of the Spirit, and not in the old way of the written code. (Romans 7:6)

Many people have become prejudiced against the Christian faith because of the way in which it has been presented to them. When zealotry and hypocrisy taint the message of Christ and transform it into a rigid set of rules from which His love and compassion are absent, it drains the power of the Gospel.

Effective Christianity only emerges when the words of Romans 5:5 ring true, "God has poured out His love into our hearts by the Holy Spirit, whom He has given us."

The Holy Spirit breathes life into Christianity, because without the Holy Spirit our religion becomes a set of dogmatic precepts that are virtually impossible to follow. True Spirit-filled Christianity is intensely personal. It is a matter of the heart and is between you and God.

While your mind is certainly important in your understanding of God, the full power of your faith is not released unless your emotions are touched, unless you have reason above the theory of your faith, and have lost yourself in the wonder, love, and praise of God that is inspired by the Holy Spirit.

CULTIVATOR OF LOVE

God did not give us a spirit of timidity, but a spirit of power, of love and of self-discipline. (2 Timothy 1:7)

The knowledge that Christ lives in you can bring about a powerful spiritual revolution in your life. It inspires your thinking, deepens your insight, gives you new confidence, creates enthusiasm, and brings purpose and meaning to your life. This is the work of the Holy Spirit, because He keeps you constantly united to the Source of true love.

If you truly love Christ, the Holy Spirit will begin to make you aware of the needs of others and you will be compelled to do something about it. Your words, your attitude, and your willingness to serve others in the power of the Spirit are the result of God's love in your heart.

The love of God works through the Spirit in your life. Then your love will inspire you to live out your faith responsibly, ably led and taught by the Holy Spirit. You will, by the help of the Holy Spirit, desire to seek nothing but the best for others. God Himself is the source of this love, which Jesus Christ demonstrated to us, and the Holy Spirit cultivates in our hearts.

INSPIRATION

*"And I will ask the Father, and He will give you
another Counselor to be with you forever –
the Spirit of truth." (John 14:16-17)*

The demands and expectations of modern life put
great pressure on people. Sadly, this often causes
them to reject the Christian faith in despair, and they
wander around in the wilderness of uncertainty and
torment.

Jesus understands human fallibility and fragility
very well. That is why He gave His disciples the gift
of the Holy Spirit, to help them to cope with the demands of life. They needed His power and strength
to encourage them when they faced such virulent opposition to their preaching of the gospel.

The gift of the Spirit is yours too, because God said,
"I will pour out My Spirit on all people" (Joel 2:28).
Jesus confirms this in the words of today's Scripture
verse.

To enable you to cope with modern life in all its
many facets and to live according to the Lord's requirements and standards, it is essential to open our
life to Jesus. Then allow His Holy Spirit to lead and
guide you according to the will of God. Then you
will be able to handle any situation, no matter how
difficult.

WALK IN THE SPIRIT

*Since we live by the Spirit, let us keep in
step with the Spirit. (Galatians 5:25)*

The essential characteristic of a person filled with the
Spirit is that he serves God wholeheartedly and does
not trust his own sinful nature. Being controlled by
the Spirit means having steadfast fellowship with the
Spirit and following His guidance in your daily life.

The guidance of the Holy Spirit is not something
that we keep for Sundays or special occasions. The
Lord gives us the fullness of His Spirit to guide us
every day, all day long. We should ask God to fill us
anew with His Spirit each morning, because the at-
tractions of the world are constantly trying to lure us
away from Him.

It is good to remind ourselves that the Holy Spirit
remains with us all day and can keep us from the sinful practices of the flesh.

If we are guided by the Spirit, our lives will reflect
the rich fruit of the Spirit: love, joy, peace, patience,
kindness, goodness, faithfulness, gentleness, and
self-control. That is why it is essential that we walk
in the Spirit.

SPIRIT OF LOVE

And hope does not disappoint us, because God has poured out His love into our hearts by the Holy Spirit, whom He has given us. (Romans 5:5)

People of different nations, traditions, and cultures across the earth testify of their love for Jesus Christ. They love Jesus Christ who died on a cross two thousand years ago. How is this possible? His ministry on earth lasted about three years, and the reports of that are rather fragmentary.

The answer does not lie in a theological dogma or religious organization. But Jesus promised His Holy Spirit to everyone who accepts Him as Lord and Savior. He has kept this promise through the centuries. The Holy Spirit lives in every person who loves and serves Him.

Remember that Christ can change your life. As you open your heart to Him, a new and unsurpassed strength will fill your soul and enable you to do those things that are pleasing to God. This change and new strength are the work of the Spirit and will assure you of Christ's presence in your life. If you have the Spirit of Christ you will know the reality of His holy presence. Love for Him will radiate from your heart and life.

THE PARACLETE

*"Unless I go away, the Counselor will
not come to you." (John 16:7)*

When we study the word *Paraclete* we begin to understand something of the wonderful gift of the Holy Spirit. Paraclete means "someone who is called in to give testimony in our favor." How comforting to know that when we are accused before God, the Holy Spirit acts as our advocate.

He inspires those who are despondent so that they can face their struggles with courage. The Paraclete helps us in times of distress and suffering, doubt and confusion. Whenever the mystery of suffering, the confusion of depression or other negative experiences enter your life, remember that you have an Intercessor at the throne of grace. Turning to Him gives you new strength and courage and helps turn the pain to victory.

The Paraclete also steps into the breach for us in times of danger. He holds our hand to keep us from stumbling. He gives us courage to walk forward even when the way ahead appears dark. He helps us deal with our imperfections and handle life's challenges. That is why it is so important for us to have the indwelling Holy Spirit in our lives.

THE SOURCE OF INSPIRATION

"But it is the spirit in a man, the breath of the Almighty, that gives him understanding. It is not only the old who are wise, not only the aged who understand what is right." (Job 32:8-9)

The foundation on which you build determines the strength or weakness of your spiritual life. If you have committed your life to Christ, your behavior should become more and more Christlike and your spiritual life should grow richer and stronger day by day.

If you are aware of spiritual poverty within yourself, you should take definite steps to develop your spiritual life. Without complete honesty, there is no challenge to develop spiritually. But to be brutally honest with yourself is not as easy as it sounds. Personal desires, changing circumstances, self-indulgence, and many other negative factors gang up to make you satisfied with lower moral standards. The results are always frustration, dissatisfaction, and disappointment.

If you open your life and heart to the Holy Spirit, you drink from the Source of inspiration and honesty. Allow Him to reveal yourself to yourself. You will discover the things that block the Holy Spirit in your life and prevent Him from working in and through you. Live in the light of God's Holy Spirit: He is the Source of all that is noble and godly in your life.

A SPIRIT OF DISCERNMENT

But you have an anointing from the Holy One,
and all of you know the truth. (1 John 2:20)

More books are being written about every aspect of the Christian faith. In many instances, age-old concepts in the Word of God are questioned and rejected. This could be very confusing and disturbing for the average Christian who runs the risk of developing doubts about his faith.

It is your responsibility to develop a personal relationship with Christ. Books and other people may be a source of help, but it is essential for you to know Christ personally, not simply to know *about* Him. You will experience the resurrected Savior abiding with you when you follow His example and live according to His commands. You will experience the Holy Spirit at work when you spend precious time in His presence, and study the truths contained in His Word.

The more sensitive you become to the stirrings of the Holy Spirit, the more He will guide you into the fullness of truth. The Holy Spirit will give you the discernment to know what is true and what teachings contradict the Word of God.

SPIRITUAL RENEWAL

*But you are a chosen people, a royal priesthood,
a holy nation, a people belonging to God,
that you may declare the praises of Him who
called you out of darkness. (1 Peter 2:9)*

The Bible tells us candidly that all have sinned and that we all fall short of the glory of God. If, however, you believe that God has forgiven your sins, it is futile to constantly remind yourself of those sins. If God has forgiven you, you must forgive yourself.

When God forgave your sins, He didn't leave a void in your life. God made you brandnew, and the righteousness that He gave you should have a positive effect on the way you live. Allow the Spirit of the living Christ to take control of your life and mind. Allow His goodness to take root and grow in your character and personality.

Disciples of Christ often struggle with this because they are unwilling to surrender themselves to Him unconditionally. A half-hearted commitment to Christ will always find excuses for vague feelings of unworthiness. If the Lord has saved you and given you His Spirit, He also fills you with His goodness that richly blesses you and all those you touch.

THE POWERFUL HOLY SPIRIT

*"We have not even heard that there
is a Holy Spirit." (Acts 19:2)*

If you are a follower of Jesus Christ, you must be an effective witness. Your worship must bring purpose and meaning to your everyday life.

Unless you open your life to the blessed working of the Holy Spirit and allow Him to take control, you will find your Christian zeal will begin to fizzle out. Your own personal efforts to live a committed Christian life are only good up to a certain point.

Regardless of how zealous you may be, you will only be able to witness effectively and successfully if you are empowered to do so through the Holy Spirit.

Those who try to serve Christ in their own strength will eventually find that their ministry lacks purpose and meaning, and the well of their faith will run dry.

Always be sensitive to the Spirit and open up your heart and life to His influence. He will enable you to serve Jesus in the way that He meant you to. This is an important subject in God's finishing school, called sanctification.

ACHIEVE SPIRITUAL MATURITY

You, however, are controlled not by the sinful nature but by the Spirit, if the Spirit of God lives in you. (Romans 8:9)

To be able to see and appreciate the greatness of God, and to rejoice in the majesty of His creation, lifts our spirit above all pettiness and spiritual immaturity.

The direction that your life has taken reveals where the emphasis in your life lies. If you seek financial success or social prestige to the exclusion of more important things, you may achieve your objective. But is it enough? Is that why God has given you life? Because you are also a spiritual being, your spirit can never be satisfied with purely material assets.

You need a dynamic relationship with the Holy Spirit, because He alone can fulfill you permanently. This intimately personal relationship with God can only be attained by faith in the resurrected Christ.

Faith in the living Christ is much more than a fleeting emotion. It is accepting His authority in all aspects of your life. It is choosing to allow His Spirit to reveal Himself through your life. With this comes a definite growth in spiritual maturity that will give true sense and meaning to your life.

REFLECT GOD'S GLORY

*Be imitators of God, therefore, as dearly
loved children. (Ephesians 5:1)*

All of us need guidance and counseling in order to reach our goals in life. Students look to their teachers, children trust their parents, employees are trained by their employers. You seek advice from your friends, or somebody that you admire serves as a role model for you.

God, through His mercy, called you to be His child. Nothing that you might have done, or could still do, will make you worthy of this gift of grace. You can never deserve it. However, there is something that you could do to show your gratitude. Through the power of the Holy Spirit, model your life on the example that Jesus Christ set for us. He lived and worked just like us and was subject to all the temptations, frustrations, joys, and sorrows that we face.

Open your heart and life to the influence of the Holy Spirit so that He can take control of your life and manage it in a way that is acceptable to God. Then you will display a measure of likeness to Christ that will glorify God.

GOD'S GREAT GIFT

*May the grace of the Lord Jesus Christ, and the love
of God, and the fellowship of the Holy Spirit
be with you all. (2 Corinthians 13:14)*

In these materialistic days, many people are unable to appreciate a precious gift of indeterminate value, which cannot be valued in monetary terms. When we reflect on the sacrifice God made on Golgotha, through Jesus Christ, for our redemption and salvation, the eternal hope that He gave us through His triumphant resurrection from the dead, the power He extends to us through the Holy Spirit, we are overwhelmed with wonder and respond with joy and praise.

There is no way that we could repay the Lord for His immeasurable love. But we could, and should, open our lives to Him so that we can pass on His love to others. Christ commanded us to love one another as we love ourselves, and as He loves us.

Because of our human weakness and frailty, we cannot do this in our own strength. Through the love of God and the grace of Jesus Christ, the Holy Spirit enables us to do His work and to spread His love among all that we touch (Acts 1:8).

THE HOLY SPIRIT AND PRAYER

*Pray in the Spirit on all occasions with
all kinds of prayers. (Ephesians 6:18)*

We long to engage in a meaningful prayer life, set aside more time for God, grow in our relationship with Him, but time and again we fail.

To triumph over Satan's attempts to distract us in our prayer time is not easy. It requires a strong will and strict self-discipline, but few people have the strength to do it. Consequently, it leads to an even bigger temptation: to stop praying because we have failed, or to slip back into prayer habits and practices that are not beneficial to our spiritual growth.

Jesus stated clearly and unequivocally that we would not achieve success without His help. He then promised the help of the Holy Spirit to those who embrace Him as their Lord and Savior, "The Spirit helps us in our weakness. We do not know what we ought to pray for, but the Spirit Himself intercedes for us with groans that words cannot express" (Rom. 8:26).

Open yourself to the influence of the Holy Spirit, be obedient to His guidance, and you will find that your prayer life will change dramatically for the better.

BAD HABITS START SMALL

Train a child in the way he should go, and when he is old he will not turn from it. (Proverbs 22:6)

We are all creatures of habit. Some habits are good, some less so, and others again are extremely bad. What we are, at this moment, is the culmination of many years' habits.

One of the most glorious facts of the gospel is that Christ breaks the power of habitual sins and sets the prisoner free. If you have a habit that is slowly destroying you, you can overcome it by acknowledging the sovereignty of the omnipotent Christ in your life.

Christ is a Master in the art of changing lives. He promises a new life to all those who follow Him and commit their lives to Him. If you recognize the truth that the Holy Spirit dwells in you, new life will flow into your entire being and you will become aware of His power that makes it possible for you to overcome every bad habit.

Habits that are acceptable to God and that contribute to your spiritual and moral well being are encouraged by the Holy Spirit, and you will know the joy and strength of your Lord Jesus, the living Christ.

CONTROL YOUR THOUGHTS

You will keep in perfect peace him whose mind is steadfast; because he trusts in You. (Isaiah 26:3)

Your thoughts influence your actions because what you think and believe is the foundation of your behavior. It is therefore imperative to discipline your thoughts and develop a positive attitude to life.

Behind every thought lies the power of desire. What you think and feel motivates your actions and responses in life. If there is conflict between your emotions and your logic, your emotions will usually win. That is why it is so important to get rid of destructive emotions and replace them with positive and creative thoughts.

The greatest force in a healthy emotional life is allowing the Holy Spirit to take control of your thoughts. If your thoughts are focused on God, He will enable you to approach life with serenity and trust, and your emotions will increasingly be subject to the sovereignty of the Holy Spirit.

You can, through the strength of Christ, control your thoughts and so experience the peace of God. While you are focusing on the kindness and grace of God, you will be assured that the Lord is in control of your thoughts and nothing can destroy your peace.

THE HOLY SPIRIT'S INFLUENCE

God, who knows the heart, showed that He accepted them by giving the Holy Spirit to them, just as He did to us. (Acts 15:8)

Most Christians admit that they experience some problems living in obedience to the commands of the Lord. Some struggle with the temptation to compromise with the sinful world. Many simply give up as their faith weakens. When others urge them to hold on to their faith, they can feel overwhelmed by the immensity of the task.

Remember that Jesus faced colossal temptations. There were moments, like shortly before He was crucified, when a compromise would have been greatly advantageous to His human welfare. If He had given in, He would have been spared the horror of the cross, but He would have robbed Himself of the glory of the resurrection, and the world of salvation.

Just as Jesus drew His strength from the Spirit of God, He offers His Holy Spirit to you to enable you to triumph over temptation and to live as He wants you to live. Open your life to the work of the Holy Spirit and remain sensitive and obedient to Him at all times. He will guide you in the ways of God. He will radically change your life for the better.

"I KNOW FOR CERTAIN!"

"No one will take away your joy." (John 16:22)

Jesus told His disciples that He was going to be crucified, and would be separated from them for a while. But He promised He would soon return to His church, through the Holy Spirit. Then they would no longer be distressed but would be filled with joy because, through His Holy Spirit, Jesus will permanently live with His followers.

The world's joy is temporary and transitory. Christ's joy is a deep well of quiet happiness and, because the source of it is the Lord Himself, it is stable and steadfast.

There may be no outward reason for joy. In the eyes of the world, it may even seem that conditions should cause us to be disturbed and desolate. But with Christ's peace that fills our lives and our hearts, we can rest assured that His eternal fountain of inner joy will never run dry and that no one can take it away.

Everlasting joy is mine. The promise comes from my Savior Himself. Therefore I rest cheerfully and peacefully in my Friend and Savior, Jesus my Lord.

YOU ARE A CHILD OF GOD

The Spirit Himself testifies with our spirit that we are God's children. (Romans 8:16)

Many books have been written about the fatherhood of God. But when all that can be written has been written, the fatherhood of God remains an experience of the soul that transcends all theories, and which enables the most ignorant person to know God as his Father.

Begin by acknowledging Christ's sovereignty, and you will know the reality and joy of His presence in your spirit. Then you will not be controlled by your old sinful nature, but by the Spirit, because the Spirit of God resides in you.

For this enriching experience to be a reality in your life, and not simply an emotional response, you need to accept God's discipline and be obedient to His holy will. God requires you to live according to His standards and with deep awareness of your unique relationship to Him.

Obedience to the will of your Father can only be achieved if you know His will. This knowledge can only be obtained by a thorough study of His Word, in which His will for us is revealed through the Holy Spirit, and by waiting upon Him in prayer and meditation.

STRENGTH IN LIVING WATER

*Then God opened up the hollow place in Lehi, and
water came out of it. When Samson drank, his
strength returned and he revived. (Judges 15:19)*

Spiritual and emotional tiredness can drain your energy and strength. If you succumb to your emotions, you are in danger of a mental, physical or spiritual breakdown. There is, however, a way of getting out of this dismal wilderness.

Turn to Jesus Christ. He is the Water of Life. He is waiting to strengthen you with living water, that wonderful, refreshing gift from God to you. Like Samson, look for the fountain of living water. The Lord offers His strength to you. In and through Him you can be revived and refreshed, renewed in mind and in spirit. You need no longer suffer weakness and lack because in Christ you have become a new creation. When you are filled with His Holy Spirit you will be revived and your life will have new meaning and purpose.

Constantly ask God to fill you with His Holy Spirit, even more so when you are at a low ebb in life. He will enable you to triumph over times of spiritual barrenness. Drink deep draughts from the fountain of faith and overcome your weakness through His strength.

BE AN ENTHUSIASTIC CHRISTIAN

And if the Spirit of Him who raised Jesus from the dead is living in you, He who raised Christ from the dead will also give life to your mortal bodies through His Spirit, who lives in you. (Romans 8:11)

Disinterest toward spiritual things is a weakness in the lives of many Christians. They have become so accustomed to sacred and holy things, that they are no longer affected by them. But we should always be enthusiastic Christians.

Some people show their enthusiasm for the things of God through physical and emotional demonstrations. However, there is a more profound and more meaningful, constructive way to be an enthusiastic Christian. That is to lead a life that is filled with the Spirit of Christ.

If the Spirit of the living Christ fills you, He permeates every facet of your life and existence. Your thoughts, your spirit, your emotions, your likes and dislikes, your fears and convictions, everything is surrendered to His control. When this happens, the holy flame of enthusiasm is lit in your life through the ministry of the Holy Spirit, and your whole life is inspired by a Power that is not of your making. Every part of you reflects the love of Jesus, even if it is sometimes imperfect. You become truly enthusiastic about Him in the life that you live for Him.

BE A COMFORTER

They approach and come forward; each helps the other and says to his brother, "Be strong!" (Isaiah 41:5-6)

Life is not easy. The ever-increasing cost of living, tense human relationships, fear of unemployment and specters of ill-health contribute to make life difficult. Unfortunately, many people accept difficult circumstances as the norm.

As a Christian, you are not guaranteed freedom from trials and problems. If you bemoan your fate and feel that God has let you down, you simply join the mass choir that sings a song of woe about the unfairness of life. And you only succeed in creating more misery and despair.

If the Eternal Spirit of the living Christ lives in you, He will prevent you from sinking into the quicksand of despair. You will look for solutions to life's problems, and will be content to cast your cares upon Christ. After all, He knows about everything. Then you will be able to live creatively and courageously.

Through the power of Christ's indwelling Spirit, you can triumph over negative circumstances, and so be able to comfort others. Then they, too, will be able to look past the negative, and see Eternity; the glorious future that God has planned for them.

SERVE HUMBLY

*"God opposes the proud but gives grace
to the humble." (1 Peter 5:5)*

If you believe that you are self-sufficient and do not need the strength and guidance of God, you will become spiritually ineffective. No servant of God can be effective if he is more aware of his own abilities than what God can do through him.

If you humble yourself in the presence of God, your spirit is open to instruction by the Holy Spirit of God. You will focus on the truth of the omnipresence and omnipotence of God and He will fill your heart and life with His presence.

But many disciples are unwilling to sacrifice their own thoughts and ideas and to allow God's wisdom and guidance to control their lives. They revel in their own opinions, and they refuse to allow the Holy Spirit to influence their thoughts.

When you humble yourself before God and are obedient to Him, you become His partner, and the service that you render to Him and your fellow man carries the mark of true Christlikeness.

THE SPIRIT GLORIFIES CHRIST

"He will bring glory to Me by taking from what is Mine and making it known to you." (John 16:14)

Christ promised that the Holy Spirit would comfort His followers when He left them. The Spirit would reveal Christ to their hearts in His triumphant, heavenly glory.

The heart's desire of the disciples was to have Christ with them continually and permanently – so as to have unbroken fellowship with Him. He was fully aware of this longing and so He promised that the Holy Spirit would reveal Himself to them in a very special way.

This was a glorious gift of grace that is still available to every follower of Jesus Christ. Everything that the Spirit receives from Christ, He reveals and teaches to God's children: He gives His love, peace, joy, and everything that could be a blessing to us. The Spirit helps us remain in constant fellowship with Jesus, helping us to get to know and serve Him better.

The Holy Spirit quietly does His work inside of us, but with dynamic power. Unnoticed, the fruit of the Spirit grows in our hearts and is revealed in our lives.

Thus, by the Holy Spirit, God, in Jesus Christ, is glorified in us.

A DWELLING PLACE FOR GOD

Don't you know that you yourselves are God's temple and that God's Spirit lives in you? (1 Corinthians 3:16)

At the very heart of every part of creation lies the glory of God. Man was created to reflect this glory by becoming a dwelling place for God. The fall into sin seemed to destroy this plan, but God never let go of His handiwork.

"You are members of God's household, built on the foundation of the apostles and prophets, with Christ Jesus Himself as the chief cornerstone. In Him the whole building is joined together and rises to become a holy temple in the Lord. And in Him you too are being built together to become a dwelling in which God lives by His Spirit" (Eph. 2:19-22).

We are God's temple because the Holy Spirit takes up residence in the purified hearts of every born-again believer and makes them a fit place for the holy God of the universe to live in.

The Holy Spirit sanctifies me and makes me God's temple, when I unconditionally hand over the keys to each room in total obedience to Him. When I open the door, God will eagerly come in (see Rev. 3:20).

JUNE

TRUST

GOD' PURPOSE

I heard, but I did not understand. So I asked, "My Lord, what will the outcome of all this be?" (Daniel 12:8)

People often find it difficult to understand God's purpose for their lives. They are confused by events and try to discover a reason for what has happened, especially when things go wrong. Their vision of the future fades, and their faith wavers.

The core of a strong faith depends on your ability to trust God completely, no matter what happens. The true test of faith comes when things turn against you; when you are tempted to question God; when you, in your despair, see no purpose for your terrible situation. When you study the life of Jesus Christ you will be impressed by His unshakeable and unconditional trust in God. Even in His darkest moments, His faith was strong enough to enable Him to fulfill the will of His Father.

If you walk hand-in-hand with God and draw your strength from Him, you will develop the ability to trust Him in all circumstances. The grace of God will enable you to deal with every situation in life, because you know that Christ cares for you and He will work everything together for Your good.

TRUST IN GOD

In Him and through faith in Him we may approach God with freedom and confidence. (Ephesians 3:12)

Trust in God can only be effective if we find ourselves able to state unequivocally, "The LORD is my light and my salvation – whom shall I fear? The LORD is the stronghold of my life – of whom shall I be afraid?" (Ps. 27:1).

Like never before, people are worried and anxious about what the future holds for them and their children. It is essential for thinking people to have a spiritual foundation on which they can base their hope and expectations. Unless you have a positive trust in a power greater than you, the future will be filled with uncertainty.

Faith in God must be intimate and personal if it is to give you hope for the future. The omnipotent Creator God has not abandoned this world, despite appearances to the contrary. His master plan for humankind will still be carried out.

This is the truth that Christ brings to a despairing world. If you place all your trust in Him, you will meet the future with an internal peace and serenity that will also inspire trust in those who surround you.

WHEN DARK CLOUDS GATHER

Surely God is my salvation; I will trust and not be afraid. The LORD, the LORD, is my strength and my song; He has become my salvation. (Isaiah 12:2)

It would be extremely naive to think that ominous clouds will not gather, darkening our lives. It would be even more futile to try to ignore them, foolishly hoping that they will just disappear. It is far better to trustingly prepare for the impending storm by standing firm in a living faith in the almighty God, who controls the storms and hurricanes.

However threatening the circumstances may be, it is imperative that you do not allow anything to usurp God's central role in your life. With Him as the center you will maintain your balance.

When your entire being is saturated by reverence and love for God, fear no longer rules your mind. Uncertainty is replaced by trust. Faith in God enables you to meet the future with joyful confidence. The ominous clouds might still be present, but you will be assured that your loving Father is working everything together for your good.

God might not disperse the clouds, but He enables you to see that even when thunderstorms threaten, He is still carrying out His holy design for your life.

Fly on the wings of an eagle

But those who hope in the LORD will renew their strength.
They will soar on wings like eagles. (Isaiah 40:31)

We so easily get bogged down by things that don't really matter. The vision of what you can become is often too easily distorted by trivialities and a restricted view of life.

A positive Christian has the ability to rise above irritations by trusting in the Lord in all circumstances and by remaining conscious of His living presence. It is impossible to be trivial and small-minded when the love of Christ fills your heart and mind. Spreading His love by the power of the Holy Spirit means being able to rise above trivialities and to reach those heights where the God of love desires all His children to live.

Regardless of your circumstances, you must never allow them to claim your attention to the extent that you lose sight of spiritual realities. These are the things that bring depth, purpose, meaning, and direction to your life. By developing an awareness of the presence of the living God, and by always trusting in Him, you will be able to rise up on the wings of eagles, and see things in their right perspective.

YOUR WILL BE DONE

"Yet not My will, but Yours be done." (Luke 22:42)

Many things come our way in life; unexpected disappointments, fiery ordeals, and often we cannot see the reason for them. But whether these are major or minor problems, we need to handle them all.

The Lord's love for us is endlessly tender and encouraging. The things He allows to happen to us are always for our ultimate benefit. He wants us to trust where we cannot see. It is not a reckless leap in the dark, but sincere trust and faith that says, "I know for certain that God's will is best for me." This kind of faith leaves the choice up to God, with the words that His Son taught us, "Your will be done!"

Our faithful prayer every day must simply be, "Your will be done!" This is the only way in which we can get to know His peace. Then we will begin to understand how His perfect will functions: always for our good, even though it does not immediately appear so. It is a wonderful privilege and blessing to be able to testify that our will is yielded to God's perfect will.

Blessed if you trust the Lord

For the LORD God is a sun and shield; the LORD bestows favor and honor; no good thing does He withhold from those whose walk is blameless. O LORD Almighty, blessed is the man who trusts in You. (Psalm 84:11-12)

God will not withhold His gifts of grace from those who are obedient to Him. God is compassionate and provides for all our needs. Often we are envious of other people's good relationships, their bright future prospects, or their exorbitant income. We too quickly forget that these things do not necessarily bring happiness.

Only a good relationship with God can bring us eternal joy. In this psalm of praise the temple choir sings, "No good thing does He withhold from those whose walk is blameless."

Things go well for those who trust in the Lord – without a doubt! So praise the Lord for the blessings that He pours out on His obedient children: grace and protection, favor, honor, and joy!

GOD REMAINS IN CONTROL

He is before all things, and in Him all things hold together. (Colossians 1:17)

Sometimes it seems as though everything is going wrong. The future appears uncertain and the present is chaotic. When problems surround you, look back over history. You will discover that through the ages nations and individuals have struggled through difficult times similar to those we face today. People were confronted with sorrow and adversity, just as we are confronted by situations today in which we have to do battle.

Before giving in to despondency, acknowledge the greatness, glory, and constancy of God. He called the world into existence, He created humankind, He has kept vigil over His creation and cared for us through the ages and sheltered us in every disaster. He is the Creator God who will never abandon His workmanship. In His vast love, He gave His Son to this world, so that whoever believes in Him shall not perish but have everlasting life (John 3:16).

Therefore, hold on to His promises; place your entire trust and faith in the living Christ. Through Him you will survive all dangers and adversity.

UNSHAKEABLE TRUST

Be joyful in hope, patient in affliction. (Romans 12:12)

When everything seems to be going wrong for you, you can be completely overwhelmed by your problems and collapse under them, or you can rashly try to solve them in your own strength. But the Lord has promised never to forsake or leave you.

Nevertheless you must have patience, because you cannot hurry God or prescribe to Him. He does things in His perfect time and way. Even if you find your present difficulties confusing, believe that God sees the big picture of your life. He is all-knowing and all-seeing. Develop an unshakeable trust in His promises and abide obediently by His judgment.

Ask the Holy Spirit to teach you to wait patiently on the Lord. Then, with childlike trust, you can leave everything in God's hands.

God wants you to experience only what is best and the most beneficial, and if this takes place in strange and roundabout ways, you should continue believing and trusting steadfastly. They who stand steadfast in affliction, receive God's most precious gifts from His treasure-house of mercy.

JESUS,
YOU LEAD THE WAY

He restores my soul. He guides me in paths of
righteousness for His name's sake. (Psalm 23:3)

Are you afraid of the future? Perhaps you are afraid
that you won't be able to do all that you can and
should do, and that robs you of your confidence. Fear
of what the future holds can paralyze your mind and
your heart.

The Lord does not want your life to be robbed of
all power and beauty because of the awful presence
of fear. You can be completely free from it if your trust
in God exceeds your focus on fear.

Remember God is omniscient, that He presides
over the past, the present, and the future, and that He
desires only the very best for your life. This will bring
such harmony into your life that no amount of fear
will be able to upset you.

Never forget that while you are moving into the
future, God is already waiting there. You can put all
your trust in Him. Then such profound peace will fill
your life that, even if storms of fear and insecurity
rage around you, they will never be able to paralyze
or destroy you.

HOLY AND OMNISCIENT

The LORD has established His throne in heaven, and His kingdom rules over all. (Psalm 103:19)

In adverse circumstances, people often begin to doubt God's power and majesty. When devastated by trouble or when tragedy strikes, their faith often wanes and the obstacles of life cause them to stumble. A study of Scripture will show you that many well-known Biblical characters fell prey to the affliction of despondency and depression.

When you find yourself surrounded by difficulties, you need to hold on to your faith and put all your trust in the victorious Christ. When it seems as if evil has gained the upper hand, meditate on Scripture and take note of what happened when God stepped into difficult situations. In the centuries since Creation, there has not been an instance when the righteousness of God did not triumph over evil.

This same God wants to be your daily companion. Let your faith be strong in all situations, and believe boldly in the omnipotence of the living Christ. He reigns supremely over everything and everyone. Let this be your strength and power in life, with all its problems and demands.

OBEDIENCE CREATES TRUST

Now it is God who has made us for this very purpose and has given us the Spirit as a deposit, guaranteeing what is to come. (2 Corinthians 5:5)

The person who disobeys God continually lives in fear that his disobedience will be revealed some day. This results in a lack of confidence; confidence which is so necessary for a purposeful and joyful life.

If you desire to have faith and trust in God, it is important that you obey Him. Such obedience is not a reluctant acceptance of something that has to be done, but a cheerful acceptance of His all-wise will for your life.

If you accept God's gift of His Holy Spirit, your greatest desire will soon be to do God's will wherever you find yourself. Initially this seems very difficult, but because of the Spirit in you, you will receive power that enables you to live a life that is pleasing to God.

One of the richest rewards of living as God expects you to, is that your trust in Him grows continually. Then you can live without fear and stop feeling inferior. As you walk in total obedience to the Spirit who dwells in you, you develop a relationship of trust with God, your fellow men, and a deeper appreciation of yourself.

FACING THE FUTURE WITH TRUST

May the God of hope fill you with all joy and peace as you trust in Him, so that you may overflow with hope by the power of the Holy Spirit. (Romans 15:13)

If you are fearful and worried about the future, you will project those very things you fear and wish to avoid into your future. Like Job you will then find yourself saying, "What I feared has come upon me" (Job 3:25).

There are many influences that could undermine your hope in the future. Perhaps you have grown accustomed to failure and you cannot imagine how you could possibly succeed. Perhaps you have allowed your faith to slip and you are not even sure about God anymore. These, and many similar reasons, could destroy your faith in God as well as the faith you have in your ability to live a victorious life.

A sure way of building your hope is to work hard at maintaining a positive faith in Jesus Christ. Strengthen the ties that you have with Him until He becomes a living, dynamic reality to you.

The more real He becomes to you, the more your fears, which have undermined your trust in Him, will change into a steadfast, constant faith in the Lord. Then you can venture fearlessly into the future.

GOD IS ON YOUR SIDE!

So we say with confidence, "The Lord is my helper; I will not be afraid. What can man do to me?" (Hebrews 13:6)

All of us experience situations where we may feel extremely uncomfortable. You might be anxious about being asked to do something that you don't feel capable of doing.

One of God's most comforting promises is found in Hebrews 13:5 where He assures us, "Never will I leave you; never will I forsake you." God lovingly invites you to turn to Him and leave all your worries with Jesus Christ. He cares for you; He is on your side; He loves you because you are His child. Jesus gave us the blessed assurance that nobody who comes to the Father through Him will ever be turned away – and that nothing can take us out of His hand!

Therefore, do not try to battle difficult situations in your own strength. If you do, you will experience the torture of stress and tension and find yourself sinking into a quagmire of doubt and despondency. Rather, take your problem to Christ in prayer and allow Him to guide you through your difficult times. Remember that there is nothing in the whole wide world that can ever separate you from His love.

JOYOUS ASSURANCE!

"Take courage! It is I. Don't be afraid." (Matthew 14:27)

Many of the Lord's children have forgotten how to live with joy and peace, and without fear. The world is overrun with wickedness, and people find little to rejoice in. They identify with the spirit of the day and forget that, as Christians, they have the ability to rise beyond the turmoil of our times.

Christian joy is not a giddy emotion that ignores evil or shrugs it off as trifling. Christ commands His disciples to remain cheerful and courageous. This implies that they should be aware of the worst that can happen and yet, with Christian optimism, hope for the best. Even when you are afraid and despair stalks you, hold steadfastly to the truth that God is still in control. Christians should be joyful and at peace because they have a living hope in their hearts.

You have the joyous assurance that the ultimate victory belongs to Christ, even though evil is rampant in the world. You can face the future with courage because you know Christ, and He has overcome the world.

GOD STRENGTHENS ME

"Blessed is the man who trusts in the LORD,
whose confidence is in Him." (Jeremiah 17:7)

Everybody is searching for peace. No one can avoid the grueling strain of life. Our modern existence is seldom peaceful, and we often experience severe stress.

If we look at the way Christ handled pressure, we see that no matter how turbulent or chaotic the circumstances were, there was always an atmosphere of peace and serenity around Him. Even in the midst of the milling, noisy masses who mocked Him at the crucifixion, His very presence and love radiated peace.

This was the result of His intimate relationship with His Father. He regularly withdrew in solitude to pray, and poured out His heart to His Father. Then He was able to return to a stormy life with the peace of heaven in His heart.

To survive the storms of life, invite the living Christ into your heart and life and give Him full control. When you know the Prince of Peace, you will be able to cope with every situation. Whatever life might have in store, you will be victorious in His strength because, "I can do everything through Christ who gives me strength" (Phil. 4:13).

CHRIST, YOUR CONFIDENCE

Dear friends, if our hearts do not condemn us,
we have confidence before God. (1 John 3:21)

Many people appear to be confident, yet behind that mask they are actually insecure and unhappy. A form of confidence comes from many sources: achieving success; dressing well; being financially secure; getting along well with people.

But true confidence depends on something more than outward appearances or human relations. It is born in the security of your relationship with Christ. It creates order, harmony, and stability in your spirit. When Christ is in charge of your life nothing can occur that you won't be able to handle successfully with His help. This creates a confidence that enables you to lead a mature, balanced life even though you might feel threatened by problems.

To approach life with trust and courage and a Christlike attitude has great practical value. When you surrender your life to Him unconditionally "I" is no longer the most important person in your world. You live in constant fellowship with Christ and as a child of the Father, by His grace, you are able to live according to His principles. Then, through the power of the Holy Spirit, you live with confidence.

SELF-CONFIDENCE

*Though an army besiege me, my heart will not fear;
though war break out against me, even then
will I be confident. (Psalm 27:3)*

Confidence is not an art that many people cultivate. We face many awkward situations that make us uncomfortable, and are frustrated by our failures in life.

It is unnecessary to become upset and unsettled by our failure to stand up for ourselves. A lack of confidence prevents you from developing your potential to the full. You should rather develop a higher regard for yourself and greater faith in your ability to achieve success.

There could be many reasons why you lack self-confidence: fear of rejection, uncertainty, inferiority and other hidden causes could all contribute to your tense outlook on life. The only way to control these destructive influences is to take refuge in a greater influence that can destroy all these things and win your whole-hearted confidence.

You meet this "greater influence" when you discover Jesus Christ as the Lord of your life and when you start loving and serving Him. When He becomes the center of your life, you will overcome your inferiority and lack of confidence. Your confidence will grow and you will lead a well-adjusted life.

INTO THE FUTURE WITH CHRIST

"Be strong and courageous. Do not be terrified; do not be discouraged, for the LORD your God will be with you wherever you go." (Joshua 1:9)

We usually face the future with mixed feelings. Will the failures of the past possibly be repeated, and will you remain in that soul-destroying monotonous rut?

What the future holds depends largely on you. You may try to avoid its challenges and continue as you have done for so many years. Alternatively, you can jump at the opportunities that come, and develop a new approach to life.

There are two ways of handling challenges. You can approach them as you did in the past, hoping for better results, but knowing in your heart that you will soon be back in the same old rut of unfulfilled expectations and doleful failures. Or you can meet the future aware of your own limitations, but also with the conviction that you serve a wonderful God who desires only victory for you.

God invites you to enter into a partnership with Him. If you step into the future with trust and faith in Jesus Christ, nothing can hold defeat or failure for you.

THE BLESSING OF DEPENDENCE

"And I'll say to myself, 'You have plenty of good things laid up for many years. Take life easy; eat, drink and be merry.'" (Luke 12:19)

The Holy Spirit comes into our lives when we realize that our happiness does not depend upon our own insignificant efforts and achievements, but upon God and God alone.

Could there be any "happiness" when you surrender control of your own life? Christ says, "Yes!" There is an extraordinary joy that touches your life bounteously and blesses it abundantly. It is a deep, authentic, serene, and sacrosanct joy that brings peace to your life. It is to be secure in God. To be assured that Somebody loves you and cares about you. That He holds you with a strong, nail-scarred hand, a sign of His great love for you. We discover true happiness when we become completely dependent upon Christ. It is like taking a blank sheet of paper, placing your signature at the bottom, and saying, "Please fill in Your will for my life, Lord!"

When we surrender to Christ, the Holy Spirit leads us to true happiness and blessing. The essence of His salvation is self-surrender and yielding; a total dependence on God. May you share in that happiness and blessing.

TRUST GOD IN THE DARKNESS

Even though I walk through the valley of the shadow of death, I will fear no evil, for You are with me; Your rod and Your staff, they comfort me. (Psalm 23:4)

Every follower of Jesus Christ sometimes face dark days of depression and despair. For a time you were aware of the living presence of the Lord. But your enthusiasm is dampened by indifference and you become satisfied with a mediocre spiritual life.

You need a fresh experience with God to drive the darkness from your life. You need His Holy Spirit to keep you from becoming insensitive and careless. He is the only One who can restore your intimate fellowship with God.

In the darkness of doubt, cling to your faith in an unchanging God. No matter how your moods or emotions fluctuate, God's love for you remains steadfast, strong, and secure. He loves you with an everlasting, unceasing love, and, even though you feel far from Him, He is always close to you.

One benefit of going through the dark places of life is the appreciation it brings when we once again experience the light and sunshine of God's love. God is able to use even the darkest experiences on your earthly pilgrimage to the benefit and blessing of others.

A LIFE BASED ON TRUST

For I have learned to be content whatever the circumstances. I know what it is to be in need, and I know what it is to have plenty. (Philippians 4:11-12)

Many timid people become slaves of everyone else's opinion. They agree with every and any viewpoint, regardless of how divergent they may be. They never have a definite opinion about anything, and prefer to remain unnoticed. They lose confidence in God and themselves. Life becomes increasingly complicated because they try to please everybody.

As a follower of Jesus Christ you have powers at your disposal that enable you to tackle life positively and constructively. Remember that dynamic discipleship is based on faith that finds expression in deeds, not on your feelings. Focus on the fact that God loves you, even though you might be experiencing the darkest time of your life. Acknowledge that He never leaves you, even though you may not be aware of His presence.

If your life is based on your faith in Christ, your confidence will gradually increase and you will overcome every feeling of inferiority. There will be no situation that you will not be able to handle through Christ's wisdom and power.

MIRACLES THROUGH PRAYER

*Praise be to the LORD, for He has heard my cry for mercy.
The Lord is my strength and my shield; my heart
trusts in Him and I am helped. (Psalm 28:6-7)*

Despite the cynicism of our age, God still performs miracles. Every time someone is healed in answer to prayer, God has performed a miracle. Every time we experience peace in our hearts after a time of tension and suffering; when a young couple falls in love; when our grief becomes bearable or is transformed to gladness – then a miracle has occurred.

Many people pray to God when they experience a crisis but when the crisis passes and their worst fears do not come to pass, they forget that God helped them in their distress.

Many Christians can testify that miracles still occur in answer to prayer. Lives have been reformed; the sick have been healed; bad habits have been conquered; broken relationships have been restored.

Hand over your problems to God in prayer today and wait on Him in faith. If there is something you need to do, do it without delay. Do not let despair overwhelm you. In the right time and in the right way God will answer your prayers and you will be astounded by the results.

FAITH REQUIRES TRUST

"Master, we've worked hard all night and haven't caught anything. But because You say so, I will let down the nets." (Luke 5:5)

Many people think that true faith is an unattainable dream. They will sometimes reluctantly admit that other people's faith is rewarded, but they doubt whether faith will work in their own lives.

The Bible provides us with ample proof of the reality and the rewards of faith in the lives of ordinary people. One of the great misconceptions about true faith is that you can simply ask what you want from God and then sit back and wait for it to happen.

The disciples once labored hard throughout the night without catching any fish. They were experienced fishermen and knew that there were no fish to catch. Yet, at Jesus' words, they let down the nets once more. According to the Scriptures they caught so many fish that the nets began to break. And so their faith was rewarded.

When you lay a matter before God you should trust Him so much that you will be willing to accept His will and be obedient to the promptings of His Spirit. Forget about what others think or say. Trust God unconditionally and He will reward your faith.

GOD IS A FATHER WHO CARES

"There you saw how the LORD your God carried you, as a father carries his son, all the way you went until you reached this place." (Deuteronomy 1:31)

Life is seldom a smooth, problem-free road. Times of peace and calm alternate with frustration, disappointment, and setbacks. These negative experiences cast a shadow of anxiety, fear, and worry over our lives.

If you yield to the temptation of being controlled by these feelings, your life will become empty and aimless. You will find yourself becoming pessimistic, thus robbing your life of its joy, purpose, and meaning.

A diligent study of the Bible and of history, as well as a careful observation of things that happen in your life, will prove that nobody escapes the disappointments of life. Your research will prove that those people who had faith in the promises of God always had the assurance that God was with them during those hard times, to help them through their difficult times through His supporting love.

When a crisis occurs in your life, the wise thing to do is to turn to God. After all, He invited us to do it, "Cast all your anxiety on Him, because He cares for you" (1 Pet. 5:7).

IN THE STRENGTH OF CHRIST

My flesh and my heart may fail, but God is the strength of my heart and my portion forever. (Psalm 73:26)

There are various factors that could cause you to feel despondent, weak, and helpless. But if you allow them to overwhelm you, the effect on your mental, spiritual, and physical well-being can be very destructive.

It is a fact that Christians must endure problems and setbacks. Indeed, Christ warned us of this, and most of His followers were severely persecuted when their faith was put to the test.

The blessed assurance that you receive from Christ is that He will never abandon or forsake you. He will provide you with the ability to successfully cope with your circumstances through faith in His strength.

This may sound like an unattainable and idealistic dream, but it can be a glorious reality in your life. You have the assurance that the heavenly Guide will always be with you. All that is expected of you is to accept His word in faith, and to remain in fellowship with Him. All you have to do is lay your fears, worries, and hopes before Him.

HIDDEN SOURCES OF STRENGTH

"Blessed is the man who trusts in the LORD, whose confidence is in him. He will be like a tree planted by the water that sends out its roots by the stream." (Jeremiah 17:7-8)

It is regrettable that so many Christians lead superficial and barren lives. Because they are not prepared to get rid of their pet sins, they fashion their faith according to their desires. Then, in times of stress, they find out that their faith is inadequate.

The unlimited resources of the living Christ are the indisputable inheritance of those who love and serve Him. They include a purposeful faith that grows stronger the more it is practiced; a deep awareness of Christ's living presence even in the busy activities of life; access to His Word that gives perspective in times of crisis.

The resources of faith are effective only when they are consistently utilized. The more you draw on them, the more effective your life and ministry will be.

If your faith is fixed on a firm foundation you will remain standing in times of spiritual drought. When your spirit reaches a low-water mark, your faith will give you wings. Despite external circumstances you will live in the land of victory because you are drawing on a hidden Source of Power.

THE CHRISTIAN'S TRUST

But as for me, I watch in hope for the LORD; I wait for God my Savior, my God will hear me. (Micah 7:7)

This world is teeming with superstitions and strange inventions in which people put their trust when planning for the future. Many are convinced that their lives are ruled by the stars; yet others seek advice and guidance from fortune-tellers; and then there are those who don't dare do business on Friday the thirteenth.

These methods, regardless of how appealing they appear on the surface, are not trustworthy. Whenever we have to deal with the unknown, there is always the fear of insecurity or failure.

There is only one way by which you can go through life with confidence, and that is through faith in God. Yes, you will still experience trouble and problems and when they do come, you will have to deal with doubt.

In your darkest moment, remember that Jesus tells you what He told His disciples, "In this world you will have trouble. But take heart! I have overcome the world" (John 16:33). This trust in Christ overcomes all superstition and offers you peace that passes all understanding.

STRONG FAITH IS POWERFUL

"Everything is possible for him who believes." (Mark 9:23)

Nothing is impossible when faith is strong. History is studded with events that were regarded as impossible at the time, but because someone refused to accept the situation, the impossible became possible. It is the person who refuses to accept public opinion who breaks through the barriers and achieves success.

To have a faith that requires your total trust, a faith you are willing to make any sacrifice for, is to have a treasure of immeasurable value. Then you know the answer to questions such as, "What is the meaning of life?" or "Why was I born?"

The power of faith is dynamic. Faith that has a wrong goal depletes its tremendous power and can cause immeasurable damage to you and those around you. When you uphold a noble faith that inspires you, the world around you will be enriched by it.

When your faith in God is a passionate conviction and His presence becomes the motivating influence in your life, you will look at life from a totally different perspective. Then you will live creatively and victoriously.

TRUST WHEN YOU PRAY

You do not have, because you do not ask God. When you ask, you do not receive, because you ask with wrong motives, that you may spend what you get on your pleasures. (James 4:2-3)

One of the most common laments we hear is, "God doesn't answer my prayers." Some people believe this is God's punishment for their iniquities. Yet others regard it as proof of the futility of prayer. Regardless of what their attitude may be, the inescapable result is always faith depleted of power. Prayer becomes a mere formality.

True prayer is to personally experience the presence of the living Christ in your quiet times and right through the day. It is the joyous assurance that the Lord keeps His promise and that He lives in you and you in Him (see John 15:4).

Such prayer becomes a faith exercise that teaches you that, as you lay your requests before Him, He will give you what you need according to His wisdom, and you will learn to recognize and accept His answers.

When your faith in Jesus Christ is strong enough to make this commitment to Him, you can rest assured that He will give you what is best for you. Gratefully accept His will and then experience His perfect peace in your heart.

WE BELIEVE WITHOUT SEEING

Therefore we are always confident ... We live by faith, not by sight. (2 Corinthians 5:6-7)

When you battle with difficulties or disappointments, or have to make decisions, do you trust God sufficiently to place yourself and your future unconditionally in His hand? Are you sure that, regardless of what He brings across your path, it will always work together for your good?

Jesus came to earth to confirm that God loves you unconditionally. His care, help, and compassion are unquestionable. And if you are sure of this, then you will be assured that Christ will not allow anything that will harm you to come your way. He wants what is best for you. With this assurance, you can trust God unconditionally in everything you undertake.

To ensure peace of mind, place yourself, your plans, and your problems in the hands of your Savior. Discuss your problems, secret fears, or important decisions with Him in prayer. Remember, you are talking to someone who, by grace, calls you His friend. He will guide you through His Spirit and take you to the place where you experience peace and tranquility.

JULY

SPIRITUAL GROWTH

ALWAYS BE YOUR BEST

I urge you to live a life worthy of the calling you have received. (Ephesians 4:1)

People tend to put on masks to hide who they really are. But Christians should be open and transparent and strive to be all that God meant them to be!

Some people see no reason to try to live a Christian lifestyle. They have tried to maintain the appearance of Christlikeness. They sinned, asked for forgiveness, and sinned again, until they felt the endless cycle made a mockery of God's forgiveness. They know who they *should be* through the mercy and power of Christ, but they also know who they *really are*, because of disobedience, sin, and self-centeredness.

There are, however, many good reasons to persevere. Jesus loves you and wants to be your Friend. The love He has for you is greater than your fluctuating emotions. His love is steadfast and constant. He puts His strength at your disposal and asks you to draw on this strength through prayer, meditation, and Bible study (see 2 Cor. 12:9).

As the love of Christ becomes an increasing reality in your life, your faith will grow and become a powerful force for good.

PROGRESS SPIRITUALLY

*I planted the seed, ... but God made
it grow. (1 Corinthians 3:6)*

If you have embraced Christ as your Savior and
Redeemer, you need to grow spiritually. To be half-
hearted in this regard, is to court spiritual disaster. A
meaningful spiritual life needs you to be disciplined
and to surrender to the will of God. This discipline
should not be a burden, but something that brings joy
to your life.

Your prayer life should reflect a willingness to pray
according to the will of God and not according to the
demands of your own heart. A disciplined prayer life
will help you develop a way of thinking that is positive and spiritual, and you will gradually understand
what Paul meant when he said, "Your attitude should
be the same as that of Christ Jesus ... " (Phil. 2:5).

Growing into the image of Christ is not a spiritual
hobby to occupy you in spare moments, but an absolute necessity if you wish to develop a dynamic faith.
Failure to grow in Christ results in a decline of your
spiritual life. You need a strong spirit, inspired by the
Holy Spirit of God, to keep your faith alive.

DISCIPLINE REQUIRED

Humble yourselves, therefore, under God's mighty hand,
that He may lift you up in due time. (1 Peter 5:6)

The extent of your commitment to God determines the quality of your spiritual life. When you understand this, you will be determined to live as God expects you to.

Commitment to God requires a willingness to go beyond an emotional experience with Him, and to become disciplined in your spiritual life. Without discipline, faith cannot grow, and you cannot effectively serve God.

Many find it difficult to prove their love for God in a practical manner. It is easy to declare your love for God when the music is stirring and the sermon inspiring. However, to live in an unsympathetic environment among ungodly people and testify to your love for God there, requires discipline that goes far beyond emotion.

Discipline means you pray when you do not feel like praying. If possible, you should have a set time and place to meet with God, and nothing should stop you from keeping this appointment. The same applies to Bible study and meditation in the presence of God. It is through discipline alone that you become a worthy disciple of the Master.

DO YOU TRULY WISH TO CHANGE?

Therefore, if anyone is in Christ, he is a new creation; the old has gone, the new has come! (2 Corinthians 5:17)

It seems as though everyone is hoping to do something *one day*. We all have the right to dream, but the tragedy is that so many dreams never become reality.

And the same is true of our spiritual life as well. The church is filled with people who will live a more devoted life *one day*, who will pray more fervently, who will diligently study the Word of God, who will strive to be a better Christian *one day*. Sadly, *one day* seldom arrives.

One of the challenges that you will have to face is whether you truly want to change! There is a world of difference between a desire to change *one day* and to really change.

The Lord never changes a person against his will. Before change can take place, there must be cooperation with the living Christ. He asks you to submit to His will before He can replace your old, rigid life with your new life. The moment you sincerely desire to change, the transformation begins, and what you once thought impossible, becomes a glorious reality in the strength of Christ.

ENSURE YOUR SPIRITUAL GROWTH

But grow in the grace and knowledge of our Lord and Savior Jesus Christ. (2 Peter 3:18)

The starting point for our spiritual life is complete surrender to the love of Christ. But it is essential that we continue to grow. Most people desire to grow: children want to be adults; short people want to be taller; weak people want powerful and muscled bodies. And they pursue the best methods for maximum growth.

Parallels can be drawn to our spiritual lives. If we do not diligently pursue the best methods, we will not grow spiritually. When the hunger for spiritual food is not satisfied, we will be handicapped and lack spiritual vigor.

Just as you care for your body, you should conscientiously care for your spirit by nourishing it with the Word of God. In this way you lay a sturdy foundation for spiritual growth. You will develop an awareness of the presence of Christ so that He can guide you as you grow in Him. Ask the Holy Spirit to open your understanding to the true meaning of His eternal Word.

Do this, and you will find that you begin to develop your full spiritual potential.

FULLNESS IN FAITH

JULY 6

*"Whoever has will be given more ... Whoever
does not have, even what he has will be
taken from him." (Matthew 13:12)*

Many people's attitude toward the Christian faith
is so apathetic that they have never been inspired to
walk in intimacy with the living Christ. And so their
faith is weak and their discipleship ineffectual.

To receive the fullness of the life that faith offers,
it should be an integral part of your life, and not just
an added extra. A dedicated Christian must be bound
to the Word of God. Ignoring the Scriptures as your
code for moral conduct may cause you to become
unbalanced, and to distort the gospel message to ac-
commodate your own personal ideology. And soon
the power of your faith is swallowed up in wishful
thinking and futile argument.

The world needs disciplined Christians who will
affirm and proclaim the teachings of Jesus, particularly His command, "As I have loved you, so you
must love one another" (John 13:34).

The discipline that is needed to live a Christian
life of love demands a strength that can come only
from the Holy Spirit. This is nurtured through prayer,
Bible study and hunger for a more profound experience with God.

FAITH IS A PROCESS OF GROWTH

Live a life worthy of the Lord, ... bearing fruit in every good work, growing in the knowledge of God. (Colossians 1:10)

It is a sad truth that many Christians make little progress in their spiritual pilgrimage after accepting Christ as their Savior. They either forsake their first love, or their faith gets stuck in a cul-de-sac.

It is relatively easy to determine whether you are growing spiritually: Is Christ becoming more real to you? Is prayer essential in your decision-making? Do you find God's will for your life in the Scriptures? Are you nearer to Christ than you were when you were born again?

It requires courage to answer these questions honestly. It can be an unsettling experience if it is not a sincere prelude to renewing your faith in Christ. Regardless of the failures of the past, the Holy Spirit will inspire you to develop an awareness of Christ's indwelling presence. There is no end to the growth and development that this will bring, because the more you are aware of Christ's presence, the greater your love for Him will become. This growth brings life-giving energy, enabling you to develop in Christlikeness, and to bear fruit in His kingdom.

CONVERSION TO DISCIPLESHIP

*"Anyone who does not carry his cross and follow
Me cannot be My disciple."* (Luke 14:27)

The decisive fact of your Christian life is not necessarily the moment of your conversion, but rather how far you have since progressed on the Christian path. Conversion is the beginning of your Christian pilgrimage, but discipleship implies growing faith, increasing love, and unconditional obedience to the Lord.

Rejoice because Christ is your Lord and Savior, and know that He will lead you along paths of increasing wonder and beauty. To begin a new life in Christ is like walking from the darkness into the light. Realizing that Christ wants to live in you and express Himself through you, opens up exciting new worlds.

Being a disciple means that we are united to the Lord and our love for Him compels us to greater obedience. Then we will be more aware of His presence in our lives.

Discipleship implies continuous growth in Christ, until He becomes the greatest motivating force in your life. Then you will discover that you can do nothing without Him, but that with Him you are able to accomplish all things.

GROW IN FAITH

Immediately the boy's father exclaimed, "I do believe; help me overcome my unbelief!" (Mark 9:24)

Many Christians encourage others with the words, "Just believe!" They assure them that wonderful things will happen if they do. But they don't tell them how to obtain such a faith. How can you and I become partakers of this faith?

You put your faith in Jesus for the common things in life, things that would probably have happened anyway. However, you need a faith that will work when storm clouds gather ominously around you.

Start with the process of developing a mature faith. Look for something small to thank God for, an instance when you believed that God answered your prayer. It is probably not something big or important, but when you remember it, your faith is strengthened in a wonderful way. Suddenly you are able to say, "God was really at work in my life."

Make a habit of recognizing the small answers to prayers. Your faith will gradually grow until you can believe God for bigger things. Don't go on yearning for a greater faith. Use that which you already have, and you will grow in faith and grace.

GROWTH IN CHRIST

We will in all things grow up into Him who is the Head, that is, Christ. (Ephesians 4:15)

Christianity without spiritual growth can never bring deep, true joy and satisfaction. When you received Christ into your life, you did not only accept a system of doctrines and dogma. You promised eternal faithfulness to Him because you believe in Him. The strength or weakness of your faith depends on your relationship with the risen Savior.

The Lord knows you better than you know yourself. You, however, can only understand Him better if you share your life with Him – and do so with all your heart. You will grow in Christ only when you stop focusing on yourself. Your own interests, ambitions and desires will sink into the background for the sake of those around you who are distressed, who are lonely and deprived.

Growing in Christ is not an exercise meant to create a comfortable religious feeling far removed from the hard realities of life. It inspires the believer to positive action.

Renew your life of prayer; rediscover the Spirit of Christ in the Scriptures. Discover that growth in Christ will lead you to new dimensions of life.

GROWTH THROUGH FAITH

"If a man remains in Me and I in him, he will bear much fruit; apart from Me you can do nothing." (John 15:5)

If your faith demands nothing from you, it is probably weak and ineffective. To be satisfied with a superficial spiritual life is a sad indication of worldliness. Prayer, Bible study, and meditation will renew your spiritual hunger and help you to follow God's will in your life.

When a Christian stops growing, the death knell of spiritual progress rings out. That is why Paul prays, "that out of His glorious riches He may strengthen you with power through His Spirit in your inner being" (Eph. 3:16).

Although salvation is a free gift of God through Jesus Christ, we have a responsibility to stay close to Him and do all we can to get to know Him better. Spiritual growth is an ongoing process to which we should dedicate ourselves wholeheartedly.

A living faith requires effort from our side because it is a real challenge to become like Jesus. But He always meets us more than halfway when our efforts are sincere, and strengthens us through His Spirit. Obediently follow wherever He leads, and your life will rise to a new level of spiritual power.

LIVE FOR CHRIST

His divine power has given us everything we need for life and godliness through our knowledge of Him who called us by His own glory and goodness. (2 Peter 1:3)

The call to live a Christian life rings out once again, but some of us are so overwhelmed by the immensity of the task that our faith falters. We tell ourselves that in our human weakness we cannot possibly meet the standards that God expects of us. And so we lose courage and refuse to even try. In this way, God is robbed of a committed disciple, and you deny yourself the joy of serving the Lord.

The mistake that you make is to rely on your own abilities to serve Christ. Rather, from the outset, devote yourself to Christ with absolute faith in your heart, and trust Him to enable you to walk in His ways.

Remember that Christ will not call you to any form of service without equipping you for it. He has set the example, and all that He expects of you is to follow Him.

If you commit yourself to Him and place your trust in Him completely, He will provide you with everything that you need to truly live.

MORE CHRISTLIKE EVERY DAY

I want to know Christ and the power of
His resurrection and the fellowship of sharing
in His sufferings, becoming like Him in
His death. (Philippians 3:10)

It is a glorious truth that believing in Jesus Christ as your Savior frees you from your sins. But you should never forget that after you have accepted Jesus Christ as the Lord of your life, the process of growth should continue. If you ignore the necessity of growth, your spiritual life will start to founder in the ocean of disappointment and despair.

In His mercy, God has put many resources for spiritual growth at our disposal, but we should be careful not to let these become an end in themselves. Fellowship with other believers is essential, but if it is not focused on Christ, it serves no spiritual purpose.

Studying the Scriptures is a source of infinite inspiration and guidance, but remember that the purpose of the Scriptures is to point you to Christ. Good works and helping those less fortunate than yourself are pleasing to God, but are only the fruits that spring from knowing Christ.

Spiritual growth can occur only when you desire to be more like Jesus. This should be the yearning of every disciple.

REACH FOR
SPIRITUAL MATURITY

When I was a child, I talked like a child, I thought like a child, I reasoned like a child. When I became a man, I put childish ways behind me. (1 Corinthians 13:11)

Many people's spiritual pilgrimage is like riding a rocking-horse: there is a lot of movement, but little progress. They never achieve mental or spiritual maturity because they allow grudges to poison them with bitterness.

We must put away the offences and grudges that we have nurtured over the years. Allowing a grudge to fester could harm your spirit and hinder your spiritual development.

As you surrender your life to Christ and become more like Him, He will enable you to let go of insults, grudges, and vexations that hamper your spiritual growth. Today you have an opportunity to grow by God's grace, to put the negative behind you, and to reach for a future of exuberant spiritual growth. God gave us the gift of the Holy Spirit to lead us to spiritual maturity. If you open your spirit to His influence and allow Him to find expression in you, a new way of living will open for you. He will help you to forgive and forget and you can then concentrate on those things that will bring you to spiritual maturity.

SPIRITUAL MATURITY

*You ... are controlled not by the sinful
nature but by the Spirit. (Romans 8:9)*

To appreciate the greatness of God and to rejoice in the majesty of His creation elevates the human spirit above the pettiness that comes from a limited view of life.

When your life seems restricted by a lack of opportunities; when you have fallen into a rut from which you just can't escape, then you begin to question the basic reason for your existence.

The direction in which your life is moving clearly shows what your priorities are. If you seek financial success or social prestige to the exclusion of more important things, you may reach your goal but lose much more.

Because God created us as spiritual beings, you can never be satisfied by worldly things. The only thing that will fully satisfy you is a dynamic relationship with the living God. This can be achieved only through a steadfast faith in Jesus Christ. This faith encompasses your acceptance of Jesus as Lord, as well as allowing His Spirit to manifest Himself through you. This will bring spiritual growth that will fill your life with new meaning.

SPIRITUAL RESPONSIBILITIES

Work out your salvation with fear and trembling, for it is God who works in you to will and to act according to His good purpose. (Philippians 2:12-13)

How serious are you about your spiritual responsibilities? You need to give your all to God and steadfastly place your faith and trust in Him. This commitment is not just an emotional experience, but a lifestyle that has practical applications of your faith to everyday situations.

You need the inspiration, wisdom, and power of the indwelling Christ. It is impossible to live as a redeemed person in your own strength. If, however, you allow Christ into your life, allowing Him to reveal Himself through you, that which is impossible to you becomes possible through His power.

Submitting to Christ so that He can work through you requires absolute surrender. Only you are morally responsible for your actions, your behavior, and your attitudes. You are responsible for the amount of time you spend in prayer; your attitude toward other people; the thoughts you harbor in your heart.

In the final analysis you are responsible for what you are. Only if you abide in Christ and He in you, will this become a reality in your life.

THE DANGER OF COMPLACENCY

For this reason I remind you to fan into flame the gift of God, which is in you through the laying on of my hands. (2 Timothy 1:6)

Complacency is a major stumbling block in spiritual growth. When you believe that there is nothing more for you to learn about the Lord and His teachings, you have reached a dangerous cul-de-sac that will lead to frustration and spiritual impoverishment.

The life of a Christian is not static, but a constant growing in spiritual awareness. Constantly focusing on your conversion without becoming increasingly conscious of the presence of the Lord in the subsequent years, effectively invalidates that experience.

Sanctification is a process. There is great joy in making Christ the Lord and Master of your life. But the effective disciple has a burning desire to know more about Him every day and to draw closer to Him. This is why he studies the Scriptures and observes the lives of those who walked the path of Christ before him.

If you do not have this desire, you may have become complacent and disregarded the challenge Jesus sets.

Ask the Holy Spirit to once again fan the flame in your life so that you can experience new spiritual growth.

SPIRITUAL GROWTH IS ESSENTIAL

*I gave you milk, not solid food, for you were not yet
ready for it. ... For since there is jealousy and
quarreling among you ... are you not acting
like mere men? (1 Corinthians 3:2-3)*

Many people believe that God is great and awesome.
In faith they accept that He is love, but refuse to allow
Him to fill their lives with that love. He promised His
power to all who serve Him, but they remain weak
and powerless; they say they believe in Him, but they
don't experience His loving presence.

Tragically, they remain spiritually immature. They
may be active in Christian work, but only cooperate
if they have their way. If they cannot be leaders, they
refuse to be involved.

The Christian way of life is meant to enrich the life
of disciples. When you start becoming spiritually mature, you develop a greater love for others. When the
love of Christ saturates you, immature attitudes such
as pettiness, jealousy, and strife are dissolved.

It is only when you have an intimate relationship
with the Lord that you receive sufficient grace to see
these negative things for what they really are. Then
you can rise above this immaturity and enjoy the
solid food that the Holy Spirit gives you.

TO LIVE FOR CHRIST

For to me, to live is Christ. (Philippians 1:21)

Too many people live aimlessly. Years pass and they have no idea what their goal in life should be, or they focus on superficial goals: they want to get rich, and enjoy worldly pleasures. But these things cannot bring real satisfaction. Real joy and fulfillment come from having a goal that pleases Christ.

If you truly love Christ, you have a good goal and the necessary strength and inspiration to bring it to pass. Your goal should be to live your life in God's grace, to His glory. You will not be spiritual only if the mood strikes you. Your faith will remain constant, in spite of your fluctuating emotions.

Living for Christ means committing your spirit, soul, and body to Him; diligently walking the road of sanctification; accepting Him as your only Redeemer and Savior.

If you live for Him, He will be alive for you and you will know the ecstasy of a life poured out before God as a thank-offering.

Accept the gift of Himself in your life and allow Him to live through you. Then for you to live is Christ and to die is gain!

WHEN YOU ARE ON YOUR OWN

Because God has said, "Never will I leave you;
never will I forsake you." (Hebrews 13:5)

Christians need to enjoy spiritual fellowship with others in order to grow spiritually. Being part of a loving community is a source of daily strength and inspiration. Trying to walk our Christian pilgrimage on our own is to expose ourselves to the danger of spiritual desolation.

But if your spirituality depends upon exuberant and perhaps emotional meetings, you might one day discover that you don't have a living faith. Then you will discover how important it is to depend on Christ and not on people.

You have to take responsibility for your own actions. When you have made certain choices, then you alone must bear the consequences and walk along the path you have chosen. Therefore, choose wisely.

When you walk the last stage of life's journey, you will be on your own. Nobody can enter the valley of death with you. And yet, you are not alone, because the Lord promised to be with you when you go into the vast unknown. As His child you have the immeasurable privilege of enjoying His companionship right through life, through death, and for all eternity.

WATER IS LIFE!

He turned the desert into pools of water and the parched ground into flowing springs. (Psalm 107:35)

Water is absolutely crucial for survival. Flora and fauna lacking water will eventually die. Water is integral to humankind's survival and success.

In the same way, your spiritual life can die unless you drink of the water that Jesus offers you. Christ offers you something that only He can give, and through that He changes the barren desert of your life into a fertile garden, the burning sand into bubbling springs.

If you want your life to have purpose and meaning, drink deeply from the fountain of living water that Christ offers you, "But whoever drinks the water I give him will never thirst" (John 4:14).

Get to know Him through what Scripture reveals of His character; through committing your life to Him; through daily prayer ; through submitting yourself to His authority in your life.

Keep in touch with the Source through prayer and meditation. Then there will be spiritual growth in your life. He invites you, "If anyone is thirsty, let him come to Me and drink" (John 7:37).

KEEP YOUR SPIRIT GROWING

*Your faith is growing more and more, and the
love every one of you has for each other
is increasing. (2 Thessalonians 1:3)*

If you are no longer enjoying your spiritual experiences you have probably allowed stagnation to rob you of your spiritual zest. Perhaps your prayer life has deteriorated and you have neglected your Bible study and quiet times with God.

A vibrant and powerful spiritual life requires constant attention. There will never be a point when nothing more is required from you. The longer you walk with the Lord, the greater your enthusiasm should be, and any tendency to grow slack should be resisted with all your might.

Your quiet times sustain and nurture your spiritual life. When you start fading spiritually, ask God for the wisdom and the courage to confess your negligence and weakness, and do something constructive about this attitude that makes you spiritually barren and unhappy.

To grow spiritually you have to become increasingly aware of the presence of the living Christ in your life. This can be the daily experience of every disciple and it will bring power and glory, joy and vigor that you never thought possible to your life.

YOUR RESPONSIBILITY

*I pray also that the eyes of your heart may be enlightened
in order that you may know the hope to which He has
called you, the riches of His glorious inheritance
in the saints. (Ephesians 1:18)*

Salvation is God's free gift to all who choose to accept it, but if you want total fulfillment and joy, you must live for Him with all your strength. People who are enthusiastic about their faith, derive much greater blessing from it than those who are lukewarm and indifferent about the truths of God.

It is our personal responsibility to develop in the spiritual disciplines. It is useless to ask God to strengthen your prayer life if you are not willing to give more time to prayer. The desire to become more Christlike is praiseworthy, but unless you are willing to spend time meditating on the life, deeds, and character of the Lord as revealed in Scripture, your desire will remain unfulfilled.

When you accept the Lord's free gift of salvation, you commit yourself to the responsibility of growing closer to Jesus.

Spiritual growth requires sustained nourishing through prayer and Bible study. These two requirements are non-negotiable if you want to remain true to your Lord and develop spiritually.

TO GROW SPIRITUALLY

*For He satisfies the thirsty and fills the
hungry with good things. (Psalm 107:9)*

Spiritual discontent can be a blessing in disguise. It is only when a person becomes discontented with himself, that he can begin to improve. Only then can he become the person God intended him to be.

Dissatisfaction with your spiritual state can be the prelude to a greater understanding of God as well as a more intimate relationship with Him. You suddenly become aware of the desire for a more realistic experience with God. There is a deep hunger in your heart to know God more intimately and your eyes are opened to your spiritual need.

The first step to satisfy your spiritual hunger is to return to the basic elements of your faith. When Christ is at the center of your life as the source of a positive, living strength, your spirit is nourished and you become inspired by a divine power that knows no spiritual hunger or thirst. "I am the bread of life. He who comes to Me will never go hungry, and he who believes in Me will never be thirsty" (John 6:35).

A BALANCED INNER LIFE

If any of you lacks wisdom, he should ask God,
who gives generously to all without finding fault,
and it will be given to him. (James 1:5)

Many people generously believe that to live a truly spiritual life, you need to live in mystical seclusion where the realities of life are either ignored or forgotten. All your energy needs to be directed toward the development of the *spiritual life*.

The lessons Christ taught along the dusty roads of Palestine were intensely spiritual, yet essentially practical. It is extremely difficult to draw a line between that which He regarded as *spiritual* and *secular*. For Him, everything – every thought and deed – was an expression of His relationship with His heavenly Father. Therefore, a true Christian does not divide his life into compartments, because all of life must be an expression of the spiritual.

The Holy Spirit sharpens our minds and makes us sensitive to discern the will of God. Paul Tournier wrote, "I wait upon God to renew my mind, to make me creative, instead of becoming the clanging cymbal that Paul spoke of." The spiritual life touches the realities of every day and enables you to look, to a certain extent, at people's problems as God does.

DON'T BE IMPATIENT

*Keep yourselves in God's love as you wait for the
mercy of our Lord Jesus Christ to bring
you to eternal life. (Jude 21)*

When some people commit themselves to Christ, an immediate transformation of their personality takes place. The weakness of their character is replaced by strength and an indescribable confidence fills their entire life. But with the passage of time the wonder and enthusiasm sometimes abates, and the spirit that was once aflame for Christ starts to dim.

When you give your life to Christ, you become a new creation, but old habits die hard. New Christians are infants in Christ, and in the process of growing, old habits may easily make their influence felt once again. Therefore it is imperative for young Christians to begin focusing on spiritual disciplines that nurture growth immediately after their conversion to Christ. The excitement of conversion should be strengthened by the pillars of Bible study, prayer, and fellowship with believers.

Without worship, prayer, and Bible study there can be no growth. It is God's desire for you to grow spiritually, but the responsibility for actually doing so belongs with you.

GROWTH THROUGH THE TRUTH

Instead, speaking the truth in love, we will in all things grow up into Him who is the Head, that is, Christ. (Ephesians 4:15)

If you ignore or undermine the necessity of growth in your spiritual life, it will not be long before you will suffer on the stormy seas of disappointment and despair. There must be growth and development, or your spiritual life will founder on the rocks.

God makes many aids available to us for our spiritual growth, but we should guard against the aids becoming goals in themselves. Fellowship with believers is necessary but if it does not have Christ at the center, it serves no spiritual purpose.

Bible study remains a source of continuous inspiration and guidance, but the purpose should always be to reveal Christ to the disciple and to glorify Him. Good deeds and charitable works are pleasing to God, but these should be the result of our relationship with Jesus Christ, and can never be a substitute for our faith in Him.

There can be spiritual growth only if your main objective is to reflect the image of Christ more and more. This should be the heart's desire of every believing Christian disciple.

PRAYER: THE CHALLENGE

*And being in anguish, He prayed
more earnestly. (Luke 22:44)*

There are enriching moments in prayer when you experience glorious intimacy with God and are filled with inexpressible joy. But true prayer often has a seriousness that touches on the deeper issues of life.

Many Christians never progress beyond prayers that simply lay their requests before God. And when they do not get the answer they want, they are disappointed.

When you pray that God will help you to grow spiritually, or show you the right way to live, or use you in His service, you will experience the full impact of the challenge of prayer.

Such prayers are essentially between you and God, but you will soon discover that they touch other people as well. When you become aware of God's presence, you bring before Him those who are in need: a child who has gone astray; a hungry, lonely person; or someone who is suffering and heartbroken.

As God lays these people on your heart, you begin to understand the responsibility of prayer. Sharing in this privilege strengthens you to live in love toward God and your fellow men.

REAL CHANGE

Do not conform any longer to the pattern of this world, but transformed by the renewing of your mind. (Romans 12:2)

Familiarity is one of the great dangers of our faith. You may have heard the gospel so many times that it no longer has any impact on you. Your heart isn't stirred by worship services anymore. Christianity no longer plays an active role in your daily life. The power, joy, and gladness that Jesus Christ promised, are just not part of your life.

Living Christianity is based on a relationship with Christ – an experience so meaningful that even the thoughts that flash through your mind are different. As you ponder Christ's teachings that love is stronger than hate, that forgiveness achieves much more than revenge, and that God really guides those who are confused, you will have a new understanding of Christianity.

If you open your heart to the prompting of the Holy Spirit, you will become aware that God is at work in your life. When He expresses Himself through your life, your Christianity becomes alive and meaningful and you change because Christ has changed your heart. This is glorious growth in the life of any Christian.

SCRIPTURAL FAITH

*"Why do you call Me, 'Lord, Lord,' and
do not do what I say?" (Luke 6:46)*

Why do so many good, church-going people experience a sense of disappointment and failure that
borders on despair? They have faithfully attended
church since childhood, and honestly feel they truly
love God in their own way. Despite this they suffer
from spiritual malnutrition. There is something important lacking in their spiritual experience.

The answer may lie precisely in the fact that they
love God in their own way, instead of in the scriptural
way. They have created a form of Christianity that fits
neatly into their lifestyle.

This private and personal version of Christianity
turns them into masters of compromise. They find excuses not to forgive; they are selective about whom
they want to love; their business negotiations are controlled by whatever suits them at that moment and
not by scriptural principles.

Scriptural Christianity means complete obedience
to God and to the standards set by Christ. Such expectations are not unreasonable, because when He calls
us, He also gives us His Holy Spirit to empower us to
live the life Christ died to give us.

SPIRITUAL VERSUS SECULAR

*"The Spirit of God has made me; the breath
of the Almighty gives me life." (Job 33:4)*

A mistake that people often make in their efforts to grow spiritually, is to think that life is divided into two separate parts: the spiritual and the secular. This gives rise to people being divided into two groups: those who try to cultivate a meaningful spiritual life, and those who follow the ways of the world.

When a follower of Christ starts thinking this way, he loses contact with reality, his faith wanes, and he becomes an ineffective witness. A truly spiritual person has a lively interest in people and in what is happening around him. True spirituality is extremely practical. Jesus was a very practical person. For Him no division existed between the spiritual and the secular.

As you grow spiritually, you should become a more balanced and stable person. If you live in the strength of Christ, you will understand that life in its totality should be lived from God's perspective and that everything is subject to His sovereignty.

AUGUST

COMFORT

COMFORT AND STRENGTH

*May our Lord Jesus Christ Himself and God our Father,
... encourage your hearts and strengthen you in every
good deed and word. (2 Thessalonians 2:16-17)*

When Paul wrote this letter to the young congregation in Thessalonica, he was deeply concerned about the persecution they were bound to face and the false teachers who would inevitably cross their path. Paul never sugar-coated true Christian discipleship. Above all, he wanted Christians to be willing to endure affliction for Christ's sake.

This prayer reveals a fatherly concern, prayed out of the earnest desire of his heart for the congregation because he could not always be with them. He prays for God to comfort them personally and to give them strength when taking a stand against false teachers.

These special promises are meant for all God's children. We too can draw near to God with confidence and ask Him to comfort us and give us strength. He is the Faithful Deliverer.

THE BLESSING OF COMFORT

*"Blessed are those who mourn, for they
will be comforted." (Matthew 5:4)*

If you are lost in sadness and sorrow, remember that your Great Comforter and Friend holds your hand firmly in His. You have a Mediator who died on the cross for you, rose from the dead, and ascended to heaven where He intercedes for your comfort.

Christ never leaves us alone in our distress. He is with you in the fiery oven, in the stormy seas, in the valley of the shadow of death.

Sometimes He completely removes the bitter cup: sickness is healed, the cross is lifted from your shoulders, the thorn is removed from your flesh, and the burden is lightened.

At other times the heavy burden remains; the cup remains bitter; but His mercy removes the bitterness from it.

Then you realize it is not what you lose, but what you have retained through grace that really matters. Trust in Him who will not allow anything to happen to us that will in any way harm us. It is He who said, "Blessed are those who mourn, for they will be comforted."

COMFORT THROUGH TEARS

Record my lament; list my tears on your scroll –
are they not in your record? (Psalm 56:8)

Tears allow us to release our sorrow and grief in a natural way. They are not a sign of weakness, but arise from love, tenderness, and compassion. Washington Irving said, "There is a sacredness in tears. They are not the marks of weakness, but of power. They speak more eloquently than ten thousand tongues. They are the messengers of overwhelming grief, of deep contrition and of unspeakable love."

Tears alleviate our sorrow and hasten the healing of our hearts. God is moved by our grief and through our tears provides us with a way of dealing with sorrow.

When Jesus wept, God showed us the sanctity of tears. He was powerful enough to remove the cause of sorrow, yet human enough to shed tears Himself.

Thank God for the healing, delivering, and purifying power of sincere tears. They soften grief, bring acceptance, and eventually lead to joy.

We also have God's promise that there will be an end to our tears. John, speaking of the new heaven and earth says, "He will wipe every tear from their eyes" (Rev. 21:4).

GOD'S RICH COMFORT

May Your unfailing love be my comfort,
according to Your promise. (Psalm 119:76)

The Lord was very aware that His disciples were heartbroken at the prospect of His departure. That is why He promised them a Helper, "I will ask the Father, and He will give you another Counselor to be with you forever" (John 14:16).

Sadness and sorrow are a reality of human life. That is why it is such a glorious comfort to hear these words uttered by the Lord Himself, who was a Man of Sorrows, acquainted with grief.

Is there lack in your home? Jesus didn't even have a place where He could rest His head (Luke 9:58). Or have you been disappointed by your friends? His friends denied and betrayed Him (see Luke 22:48, 58).

Are you mourning the death of a loved one? Remember that Jesus cried at the grave of His friend Lazarus (see John 11:35).

In the midst of our adversity and distress; our poverty and lack; our cares and worries, Someone who understands and cares comes to us with the words, "Blessed are those who mourn, because they will be comforted." Trust God to lead you from bitterness to joy by His compassion and grace.

GIVE YOUR BURDENS TO CHRIST

Cast all your anxiety on Him because He cares for you. (1 Peter 5:7)

A businessman, facing many difficulties, was asked how he managed to sleep in spite of all his worries. He replied that he relinquished all his problems to God, saying, "Indeed, He who watches over Israel will neither slumber nor sleep" (Ps. 121:4), and he saw no reason for both of them to stay awake all night!

His reply reminds us to trust God under all circumstances. Jesus promised never to abandon us (Heb. 13:5). He invited those who are weary and overburdened to come to Him for rest, and He will never turn away anyone who comes to Him.

God does not necessarily offer you instant solutions, or make all your problems simply disappear because you pray. But if you place your faith and trust in God and confide in Him in prayer, you will experience the peace of mind that will make you sensitive to the guidance of the Holy Spirit. He will enable you to think clearly and act positively. In His strength you will be able to handle your problems in line with the will of God.

GIVE YOUR PROBLEMS TO JESUS

The troubles of my heart have multiplied;
free me from my anguish. (Psalm 25:17)

Few things have such a negative effect on your spiritual, physical, and emotional well-being as problems and worries. They play on your mind to such an extent that your mental abilities may be impaired. In many cases this results in people becoming spiritual and physical wrecks.

When Jesus called those who are weary and over-burdened to Him, He did not guarantee exemption from problems, nor did He promise that all problems would disappear instantaneously. Instead, He offers to share your burden and teach you how to cope with it so that you can find peace of mind.

You cannot predict what setbacks you will face, nor how serious they will be. But it is important that you prepare yourself to handle these problems when they arise.

To maintain a healthy balance and harmony in your mind, it is essential to develop a healthy personal relationship with the living Christ. Remain near to Jesus through faithful prayer and meditation. Then, when problems strike, you will find that He will be with you to help you overcome them with peace in your heart.

HE CARRIES US
DAY BY DAY

*Our God is a God who saves; from the Sovereign LORD
comes escape from death. Surely God will crush the
heads of His enemies, the hairy crowns of those
who go on in their sins. (Psalm 68:20-21)*

In the presence of God, meditate on the image presented in this passage. Place yourself in David's position. When you begin to talk to God about your needs and concerns, imagine that God's arms surround you with loving protection and allow His encompassing presence to comfort you.

What images do you have in your mind when you pray? Do you have a picture of a loving Father who hears the cries of His child? Or of a mighty warrior who has charge over countless legions of angels who are ready to do His bidding?

Your answer will probably depend on what it is that you are asking for at this time. David's prayer provides an intimate image of God who carries His child in His loving arms.

TRUST IN GOD

Let us hold unswervingly to the hope we profess,
for He who promised is faithful. (Hebrews 10:23) ·

At times, everything looks hopeless and bleak. Your dreams are in shreds, hope has died, and nothing seems to work out right for you. Then we are greatly tempted to look for something or someone to blame, or to give up all hope and throw in the towel. This causes immeasurable damage to your mental and spiritual welfare.

In this state of dejection, we become easy prey to the tempter whose main aim is to drive a wedge between our Heavenly Father and us.

When you feel dejected, it is important to remember that Jesus has promised to be by your side throughout your life.

Jesus invites you to cast your problems upon Him and to trust in Him when you are in distress. Study the Gospels and see how compassionate and loving He was toward people, and draw hope and comfort from that.

If you open your heart and life to the Holy Spirit, He will be by your side and guide you into the will of God.

SHARE ONE ANOTHER'S BURDEN

Then they sat on the ground with him for seven days and seven nights. No one said a word to him, because they saw how great his suffering was. (Job 2:13)

Job's friends did not know why he had to suffer so terribly, but nobody can doubt the sincerity of their sympathy. Without saying a word, they sat with him for seven days and nights. Their wordless presence was a balm for Job's distressed heart.

Job's faithful friends show us the value of sympathetic support for those who are suffering. When a loved one suffers, you might not know what to do to alleviate his or her pain. Suffering causes frustration and torment of the soul.

Do not allow distressing circumstances to undermine your faith in the omnipotence of God. Keep God's love in the center of your thoughts and, with Job, say, "Though He slay me, yet will I hope in Him; I will surely defend my ways to His face" (Job 13:15).

Hold on to your faith in the face of every kind of adversity. Your sympathy will increase and you will become a source of strength to others who suffer – even if you have no words to say. Just knowing that you are there and that you care will greatly comfort the suffering soul.

THE COMPASSIONATE JESUS

*When He saw the crowds, He had compassion on them,
because they were harassed and helpless, like sheep
without a shepherd. (Matthew 9:36)*

Compassion is a distinctive characteristic of Jesus' personality. It flowed from the center of His heart and filled His teachings. People enjoyed listening to Him, and walked many miles to hear Him. The brief record that we have of what He did and taught in three years, reveals the depth of His wisdom and the uniqueness of His revelation of God the Father.

The love that permeated His teachings not only touched people's minds, but their hearts as well. They felt His love for them and responded by opening their hearts in love to Him.

Because the eternal Christ still lives today, His compassion and sympathy are just as much a reality today as when He walked on earth. We rejoice in the truths He preached, and our hearts are warmed by the reality of His love for us.

If life has disappointed you, or if you have failed and are filled with despair, with no idea where to turn for inspiration and strength, remember the compassion of Jesus. In the power of His love He encourages you to persevere and to rebuild your life.

FAILURE IS NOT PERMANENT

He who was seated on the throne said, "I am making everything new!" (Revelation 21:5)

Failure is a very depressing experience. Ideals are shattered, hope dies, and dreams become nightmares. Your self-image receives a blow and nothing worthwhile seems to remain. You are left with a nagging sense of your own inability.

It is beneficial at such times to do some honest soul-searching. Evaluate your life with objectivity and honesty. Confront the truths that caused your failures and deal decisively with them.

Remember that, however big your failure, it is not final. Admit that you have made a mistake and ask for forgiveness where necessary. You may need a new vision and renewed determination. Whatever your need may be at the moment, you remain a failure only as long as you accept yourself as such.

We have all known failure at one time or another. But if you are a disciple of Christ you have His unsurpassed power at your disposal to renew you. He makes everything new!

WHEN SORROW KNOCKS

"I am with you always, to the very end of the age." (Matthew 28:20)

One of the most common causes of sorrow is the death of a loved one. For many years you shared your life with a dear one, and now he or she has passed away and you feel completely alone and totally lost.

Bear in mind that you are really grieving for yourself because your loved one is with the Lord. Don't grieve uncontrollably for those who go ahead of you. They are now living in the fullness of God's presence.

Another cause of sorrow is when a family member does something that brings shame upon all the others. This is a very bitter experience and those who endure it feel as if the whole world is condemning them. But remember that most people are sincere in their sympathy because they are acutely aware of their own vulnerability.

The wise thing to do is to start reconstructing your life, without paying attention to what others say or think.

Death and shame are not issues that you should handle on your own. Christ experienced both, and He triumphed over them. And He will help you to do so, too.

An understanding Savior

Because He Himself suffered when He was tempted,
He is able to help those who are being
tempted. (Hebrews 2:18)

Never allow self-reproach to discourage you from living the life Christ has intended for you. Perhaps you have a hidden moral weakness that you have been trying to overcome for a very long time. You sincerely long to break its hold on you, but you fail every time.

You may feel despondent because of your failures, but Christ knows you better than you know yourself, and He still believes in you. He knows the intensity of your temptation, because He, like you, faced temptation. He triumphed over every temptation, no matter how severe, and in His great love He wants you to do the same.

The fact that He understands doesn't mean that He condones your weakness. But He places a power at your disposal that makes it possible for you to triumph over every temptation in His Name.

This power is the gift of His indwelling presence that He gives when you love Him and surrender to Him. When your love for Him controls your whole being, you start living in victory.

A FRIEND FOR THE LONELY

"I am the only one left." (1 Kings 19:10)

Sometimes you feel dismally alone in the midst of a crowd of people. You might have been used to the privacy of your own room, but suddenly have to share a ward with others. You find that even though you are among people, you still feel isolated.

This kind of loneliness is experienced by everyone who is separated from a familiar environment, and it is accentuated when the new surroundings are unsympathetic. A young person leaving home for college or an elderly person moving into a home for the aged might feel very lonely and vulnerable.

The secret of overcoming loneliness lies in knowing that the living Christ is with you at all times. Constantly affirm His presence in your heart and your spirit. Be assured that He is with you in the tough times of life.

Wherever you are, you will probably find other committed children of God wanting to fellowship with you. The most important thing to remember is that your heavenly Friend is always there for you.

GOD REMAINS FAITHFUL

What if some did not have faith? Will their lack of faith nullify God's faithfulness? (Romans 3:3)

Let us remember the wonderful and comforting truth: God remains faithful! If someone lets you down, you feel deeply hurt and disillusioned. You probably loudly declare you will never trust anybody again. Although you mean every word, this is not usually possible, because our whole life is based on trust.

Human nature is very unreliable and disappointment is common. People do not usually disappoint you intentionally, but it is something we learn to expect because of our imperfect and sinful nature.

The only Unchanging One in an ever-changing world is God! His promises are certain and unfailing. Since the beginning of time, people have proclaimed His faithfulness. Even though He does not always act according to our plans and desires, He proves in His own, unique way that He is faithful and true. He brings His plans to pass in the lives of those who trust Him unconditionally.

When clouds of doubt and sorrow threaten and when it seems as if everybody has disappointed you, hold tightly to God's trustworthiness. The clouds will disappear and you will be able to rejoice in God's faithfulness once more.

GOD'S GRACE

In all your ways acknowledge Him, and He will make your paths straight. (Proverbs 3:6)

Life can suddenly become filled with problems. Regardless of their source, they dominate your life until you have found a solution.

Discussing a problem with a trusted friend often puts it in the right perspective. There are, however, some people who delight in talking about their problems, while secretly hoping never to find a solution, because then they won't have much left to talk about.

If you are experiencing a problem and sincerely seek a solution, direct your thoughts to God and don't focus on the problem. You cannot find a solution to your problem if you do not allow God to assist you.

Tell God about your problem, and continually confirm His might. Allow Him to create order in the chaos and to give you the right solution. When God becomes more important than your problem, you will be fueled by a spiritual power, because God is occupying His rightful place in your life. You will find solutions to your problems and by His grace you will be able to live victoriously.

A REASON TO LIVE

"Because I live, you also will live." (John 14:19)

Many people wonder whether life is worthwhile. Fear of an unknown future paralyzes them, and they tend to have pessimistic thoughts.

Despite how cheerless the future may appear, remember that life is precious and your life and the future are both in God's hands. The Christian's life is not ruled by blind fate. God is in control of every situation in which you find yourself. He knows your needs and is always ready and able to provide for you.

As your faith grows and you begin to trust Him more, you will begin to realize the joy of life in Christ and be comforted by the presence of the unfailing love of God. He is the Rock upon which you can build your life.

Through His death and resurrection, Jesus not only gave you life, but also a reason to live. Through His Holy Spirit He provides you with the means to cope with life. Choose life and live it in the abundance of Jesus Christ, always honoring Him.

DON'T DESPAIR

*"In this world you will have trouble. But take heart!
I have overcome the world." (John 16:33)*

Sometimes even God's children start to despair. Has God turned His back on this ailing world of anarchy and chaos? Certainly not! God never abandons the work of His hands. It is still His world and He is still in control. In His good time the light will break through.

In Genesis 42 we read about the calamities Jacob faced. The country was in the grips of the severest drought in living memory, his beloved wife, Rachel, died in child birth and he believed his favorite son, Joseph, was dead. On top of this, Simeon was a prisoner in Egypt, and his darling youngest son, Benjamin, was being taken from him.

Jacob could not see that it was necessary to relinquish Benjamin so that he could experience God's miracles. He thought that Joseph was dead, but God was using Joseph to feed all who were devastated by the famine.

When times are dark, remember, God is alive; He is in control; He cares for us. "We know that in all things God works for the good of those who love Him, who have been called according to His purpose" (Rom. 8:28).

PEACE IN THE MIDST OF CHAOS

But in keeping with His promise we are looking forward to a new heaven and a new earth, the home of righteousness. (2 Peter 3:13)

In times of crisis some people tend to lose all courage and hope, and collapse in what they perceive to be a lost battle against insurmountable problems. But to everyone who believes in Him, Jesus offers a life of abundance.

This promise encompasses your situation here and now, and everything in your whole life. Because He conquered sin and death, Christ has prepared a place for all the faithful in the eternal glory of the kingdom of God.

The Lord offers you His Holy Spirit if you surrender yourself to Him. It is His Spirit who gives you the ability to handle life's problems successfully in the certain knowledge that He will not forsake or abandon you. As Paul says, "If God is for us, who can be against us?" (Rom. 8:31).

Whatever your circumstances may be, remember that Jesus is constantly at your side to guide and help you. Place your trust in Him as He leads you, and remember that He is guiding you toward God's eternal kingdom where there is only harmony and peace.

LONELY,
BUT NEVER ALONE

*How great is the love the Father has lavished on us,
that we should be called children of God! And
that is what we are! (1 John 3:1)*

The love of family and friends is always a great source of comfort and joy. To have someone with whom you can share your life is one of God's greatest gifts of grace. No wonder, then, that parting from a loved one fills us with sorrow and loneliness.

But remember, you are never alone, because nothing in all of creation can separate us from the love of God in Jesus Christ (see Rom. 8:38-39). The Lord assures us that He will never forsake us and that He will be with us all our days (Heb. 13:5 and Matt. 28:20). These are promises that you can hold on to and draw courage and strength from in all circumstances, especially when tragedy comes into your life and you are at your most vulnerable.

To reaffirm the assurance of God's promises and presence, spend time in His presence in prayer. Share your fears and worries with Him, as well as your loneliness and vulnerability. Christ is not only the Lord of your life, but also your Friend. He chose you to belong to Him through His grace.

THE EXTENT OF GOD'S LOVE

"I have loved you," says the LORD. "But you ask, 'How have You loved us?'" (Malachi 1:2)

If we tried to count all the ways in which God loves us, we would reach infinity and only have just begun the list. Nevertheless there are many people who, for a variety of reasons, do not comprehend God's love.

In the midst of personal set-backs and tragedies, in hardships and disappointments, many people blame God for the situation they find themselves in. They question God's wisdom and love for allowing such things to happen to them. In many cases, people turn their backs on God because they judge Him by human standards.

Tragically they do not see that the disasters of this world cannot be ascribed to a lack of love in the Father or the Son, but to the foolishness of man. God gave us freedom of choice and we, as human beings, selfishly misuse it.

The love of God is revealed in His abundant blessing, His all-powerful forgiveness, His mercy, His promise of eternal life, His comfort, His gift of the Holy Spirit and above all, the sacrifice of Jesus Christ on Golgotha. Do we need more proof than this?

IF YOUR BURDEN IS HEAVY

"I despise my life; I would not live forever. Let me alone; my days have no meaning." (Job 7:16)

When you are feeling dejected, it is good to go and do something that will cheer up someone else who is down-hearted or lonely. It is impossible to make someone else happy without easing the pain in your own heart.

Take a good look at the world around you: there is always someone whose burden is heavier than yours, whose sorrow is about to overwhelm him. Perhaps there is someone in your circle of friends who requires help that only you can give. It might just be possible that your own sorrow equipped you for greater and more effective service to others.

God can use your depression and despondency to enrich the lives of those around you. Share your burdens with Him – He will never burden you with a cross too heavy for you to carry. Get ready to experience how He lifts the burden from your shoulders when you serve and love your fellow men.

Never fall into the pit of self-pity. If your love for God is true and sincere, you will love your fellow man and serve those God sends across your path.

THE WORD STRENGTHENS

*Open my eyes that I may see wonderful things
in Your law. (Psalm 119:18)*

Disillusionment and dejection are common these days. Emotional ups and downs result in a precarious and unstable existence. Many people have a melancholy outlook on life that negatively influences their plans, behavior, and decisions.

In order to *live* and not merely *exist*, develop a positive attitude. When everything goes well, enjoy life and remain cheerful. When things take a turn for the worse, try to identify where things went wrong and do what you can to improve the situation.

You need a strong faith to deal with problems and overcome stumbling blocks. Such faith comes through prayer, when you seek the help of the living Christ. But to prevent you from falling prey to discouragement and pessimism, something more is required.

Continuously turn the Scriptures for testimony of the wonderful work of the almighty God. You will find example upon example of the ways in which ordinary people overcame tremendously hostile forces in the Name of the Lord. Draw comfort from the Word and through the incarnate Word, Jesus Christ, you will be able to triumph over any adversity.

WHEN EVERYTHING SEEMS LOST

*"Do not grieve, for the joy of the LORD
is your strength." (Nehemiah 8:10)*

There are many times when the sky above us is over-cast with ominous clouds. The loss of a loved one, a friend, or even a pet can cause sorrow. To be separated from someone who has been an intimate part of your life can be traumatic.

When this happens, many people have difficulty filling the void and they fall into despair. This can severely damage their mind, emotions, and spiritual life.

It would be utterly foolish to expect you not to experience sadness when separated from someone you love, yet it is important to remember that with the help of Christ Jesus you can handle your sorrow with dignity.

It is unthinkable that God's great heart of love was not grieved when His Son was sacrificed on the cross, or that Jesus was not grieved when He had to part with His disciples. But the love, joy and peace of God sustained Him. And this is still the grace that helps you overcome sorrow.

Surrender to the risen Christ. Allow His strength to support and encourage you.

EXCESSIVE CONCERN

"Therefore do not worry about tomorrow, for tomorrow will worry about itself. Each day has enough trouble of its own." (Matthew 6:34)

Many people like to sit and ruminate over their problems. Life has overwhelming responsibilities and is very demanding. Sometimes our priorities become distorted and we lose hope. Because of insufficient faith, worry flourishes in this chaotic breeding-ground.

The first step to overcome worry is to clearly identify its cause. Continuous worry crushes your heart and mind, bringing disastrous results.

Outline your worries by writing them down – clearly and simply – on a piece of paper. Then look at them calmly, pray about them and scale them down to their real size. Prayerfully confirm that God is in control of the situation that has developed and that worry will no longer affect your tranquility and peace of mind.

If you take this creative step today, you will discover that you are prohibiting worry and anxiety from clouding your future. The secret is to carry your burdens to God in prayer. And that means being conscious of Christ's presence so that He is more real to you than your worries. Christ is all-sufficient for our needs, today and tomorrow.

PEACE IN THE EYE OF THE STORM

While they were still talking about this, Jesus Himself stood among them and said to them, "Peace be with you." (Luke 24:36)

Life is sometimes filled with frightening and horrifying experiences that cause you stress and inner conflict. You become moody and discontented and your health begins to suffer. Your peace vanishes.

You need to develop inner reserves from which you can obtain strength in situations fraught with stress. The most important source of strength is the peace that Jesus Christ offers to those who love and serve Him. To live with His peace in your heart will free you and enrich your life.

When things go wrong and stress develops, purposefully refuse to be swept into its current. Guard against bad temper and irritability. Deliberately choose to remain tranquil by controlling your thoughts.

Step aside from the troubles for a while. If at all possible, spend time alone with Christ, even if only for a few minutes. Affirm your dependence on Him. Accept that His peace is available to you.

Very soon your spirit will become calm and His peace will refresh your life like the refreshing rain.

JESUS HELPS THE DESPONDENT

"I have had enough, LORD," he said. "Take my life; I am no better than my ancestors." (1 Kings 19:4)

How often have you felt like giving up? Your plans go awry; your problems seem insurmountable; you just overcome one crisis when the next is upon you. Your good intentions are misinterpreted, you are blamed for things you didn't do; you are treated unjustly. You start wondering what the purpose of life is all about.

When this happens to you, think back to when Jesus was alive. The Son of God – He who was born because of God's love for the world and whose life exemplified the greatest love of all time – was despised and forsaken by people. He was crucified for our sins and to Him belonged the sorrow that brought us peace.

Despite injustice Jesus never hesitated or stumbled. He had a divine mission to complete. By placing His faith in God, He showed the world the meaning of love and forgiveness.

When you are feeling down, turn your heart and mind to Christ who knows and understands your suffering better than even you can. Place your trust in Him and He will lead you from the darkness of your own despondency into His marvelous light.

JESUS CARRIES YOUR BURDEN

"Come to Me, all you who are weary and burdened, and I will give you rest." (Matthew 11:28)

Many people live under incredible pressure. Tension and stress take their toll on young as well as old. People of all ages are exposed to all kinds of temptations that only result in disaster for them and their loved ones.

Professional counseling, medical treatment, and medication have become common remedies for people suffering from stress. In most cases, these are only temporary measures that are merely a crutch to help people stumble through life. And still the tension keeps increasing.

There is only one infallible way of coping with tension and stress, and that is Christ's way. He, who also lived and worked under immense pressure, offers you the peace of God that surpasses all understanding. It is a peace that banishes all anxiety and fear and gives you the ability to cope with life in the strength of the Master. Accept His gift of peace and rest.

THE TITUS-MINISTRY

*But God, who comforts the downcast, comforted us
by the coming of Titus, and not only by His coming
but also by the comfort you had given
Him." (2 Corinthians 7:6-7)*

The world is teeming with people who are downcast, and things are made worse by the prophets of doom who delight in forecasting disasters.

When people are at their lowest, they need someone who can encourage them. Whether you are aware of the cause of the person's depression or not, you will be able to find something positive and encouraging to say if you really want to comfort them.

A true follower of Jesus Christ will always try to be a stabilizing factor in a difficult situation. Even though others are prophets of doom you can bring confidence and encouragement into the lives of those who are insecure and fearful. If you want to practice the Titus-ministry, which brings stability to insecure, discouraged people, you need spiritual qualities that can only be obtained through continuous fellowship with the living Christ.

Then not only will your life be enriched, but you will also bring comfort and blessings into the lives of others. This is a glorious and important ministry, because by God's grace you encourage and inspire those who have lost hope.

FAITH CONQUERS DEPRESSION

"But for you who revere My name, the sun of
righteousness will rise with healing
in its wings." (Malachi 4:2)

Depression is an ailment that destroys the soul. Not only is it an illness of the mind, it also affects your physical and spiritual well-being, limits your vision of the future, and negatively influences your general outlook on life. The causes of depression are numerous and include fear, anxiety, illness, financial instability, and loneliness, to name but a few.

You may attempt to fight the condition with medication, but the effect will only be temporary. Sooner or later the effects will wear off and your condition will return, often with a vengeance.

The only way to effectively fight such an emotional disruption is to turn to Christ and to open yourself to His love and healing influence. Accept Him as the Lord of your life and unconditionally put yourself in His care. This will require immense faith, but when Jesus takes control of your life and guides you on the path you have to take, you will find that, because of your obedience to Him, you will be filled with self-confidence and well-being that only He can give you.

GOD KEEPS HIS PROMISES

"He will never leave you nor forsake you." (Deuteronomy 31:6)

It is good to know someone who is reliable and to whom you can turn at any time. You probably have a number of friends like this and yet sometimes the friend you trust the most might disappoint you because he is unable to meet your urgent needs.

Our Lord and Master is so reassuringly different. If you need comfort, the Lord will comfort you. If you need guidance, the Lord will guide you. If you need inspiration for a difficult task or decision, the Lord will inspire you, if you allow Him to do so.

Are you tired, troubled, or confused? Does the road ahead seem to be strewn with problems, concerns, and troubles? Ask the Lord to help you and you will discover the truth of His Word as it is recorded in our text for the day. He will grant you peace and joy in abundance. If you ask Him, you will discover that the Lord is as faithful as He has promised in His Word.

SEPTEMBER

WISDOM

KNOWLEDGE VS WISDOM

The LORD gives wisdom, and from His mouth come knowledge and understanding. (Proverbs 2:6)

Knowledge is a wonderful thing and you can never have enough of it. Those who specialize in a particular field of knowledge to better serve their fellow men deserve our appreciation.

The Scriptures declare that our God is a God of profound knowledge (1 Sam. 2:3). A thirst for knowledge is actually a yearning for a deeper understanding of God and His ways.

Knowledge is insufficient unless it is focused on God and an all-encompassing love of life. As you grow in an intimate understanding of God, your knowledge will be transformed into wisdom.

Many intellectual people fail to develop meaningful relationships with others. They have no control over their behavior and emotions because they do not appreciate the value of their fellow men.

The Word of God teaches us, "The fear of the LORD teaches a man wisdom" (Prov. 15:33). To honor God and to build an intimate relationship with Him through Jesus Christ is the first step in transforming knowledge into wisdom. Maintain fellowship with God through prayer, Bible study, and meditation.

SPIRITUAL WISDOM

The fear of the LORD is the beginning of wisdom;
all who follow His precepts have good
understanding. (Psalm 111:10)

An education is definitely an advantage in life. It is, however, possible to be highly educated yet lack spiritual insight. Sanctification is always more important for the Christian than secular education.

You may be disappointed about not having been able to obtain a good education and feel inferior to others because you think they are cleverer than you. Remember that your lack of a higher academic education need not affect your spiritual growth and service for the Lord. A person who is in the process of developing spiritually is closer to the heart of God and is, therefore, more skilled in understanding God's ways than the person who is intellectually brilliant, but denies the existence of God.

A spiritual person has discovered the true Source of wisdom. He has peace and inner strength that comes from fellowship with the Holy Spirit, and lives his life with contentment and purpose. Therefore, spend time with God, allowing the fragrance of His life to permeate your life so that you can serve Him in truth, and so that His wisdom, peace, and strength can flow through you.

PRAYER FOR DISCERNMENT

Your righteousness is everlasting and Your law is true. Trouble and distress have come upon me, but Your commands are my delight. Your statutes are forever right; give me understanding that I may live. (Psalm 119:142-144)

The trials and tribulations of life often force us to turn to someone or something for help. We tend, however, to look for a sympathetic ear first of all when wrestling with a problem.

The Psalmist knew it was best to turn to God for wisdom and discernment. He asked God, "Give me understanding that I may live." He knew that God's plan for his life would preserve him from wrongful actions and would destroy the path of the foolish. Therefore, he chose to delight himself in God and to uphold His statutes.

Perhaps you are also wrestling with a difficult problem. God promises to grant us wisdom if we ask Him for it (James. 1:5). Pray to God for discernment and wisdom in your struggle and ask Him to teach you what you need to know, so that you can apply His wisdom to your situation.

LET WISDOM CONTROL YOUR LIFE

"I pray ... that Christ may dwell in your hearts through faith. And I pray that you, being rooted and established in love, may have power." (Ephesians 3:17-18)

If you are aggressive, you reveal a restless soul and probably experience bitterness, frustration, and failure. Remember that life is not out to get you. Such thinking is often the result of disappointment and goals that have been blocked.

It is important for your life to be controlled by godly wisdom. This wisdom is not the result of education but it comes through the Spirit. As you seek for a deeper understanding of God through prayer and Bible study, you develop a wisdom that can come only from Him.

This wisdom affects your whole life. Your values are no longer determined by human standards, but you will see people, circumstances, and situations as God sees them. Disciplining yourself to look at life from this godly viewpoint will give you a new sense of purpose and a changed lifestyle.

When you are in harmony with God, aggression will dissipate because you no longer take offense so easily or feel sorry for yourself. You will experience the joy of cooperating with others through the wisdom God gives you.

FROM THE STAR TO THE WORD

Your word is a lamp to my feet and a light for my path. (Psalm 119:105)

The wise men were guided by a star, but when they arrived in Jerusalem, the Word of God lighted their path to Christ. In Jerusalem everyone was expecting a King, but they did not know where to find Him. The teachers of the law turned to the Word of God.

We find the wise men with their star, but without a Book and the people of Israel with the Word, but without their King. So they returned to the Word with its irrefutable authority and in Micah 5:2 read, "But you, Bethlehem Ephrathah, though you are small among the clans of Judah, out of you will come for Me one who will be ruler over Israel."

The star is subservient to the Word. The truth of the Word remains when the glamor of the spectacular fades. The journey to finding Christ must be based on the Word of God. The stars without the Scriptures leave us with an insatiable longing for eternity but without any clear direction. The Word guides us to the King.

DECISIONS, DECISIONS!

So whether you eat or drink or whatever you do, do it all for the glory of God. (1 Corinthians 10:31)

Making decisions can be a burdensome task. What you decide can have far-reaching consequences for your own life as well as for the lives of people who are dependent on you. That is why some people try to avoid their responsibilities while others make reckless or selfish decisions.

To ensure that you do not become ensnared in these traps, you should take all your concerns to God in prayer. Lay your problems, doubts, and fears at His feet and talk to Him about your plans and thoughts for the future. Leave the matter to Him and ask Him to guide you in every decision that you have to make, so that you remain in His will.

If you are willing to trust the Lord unconditionally, you will find that He will open doors for you in His own wonderful time and way, and will guide you on the path that He has chosen for you.

Remain in the presence of the living Christ, and continually aspire to please God and you will find that you make the right decisions because God lovingly guides you.

SAY "YES!" TO LIFE

*"I have come that they may have life,
and have it to the full." (John 10:10)*

SEPTEMBER 7

The past may have been a tale of frustration and increasing bitterness, and you may feel that your life is uninspiring and dull, and that nothing you do is constructive or worthwhile. You may find little reason for hope in either the present or the future.

But the future belongs to you and you can do with it whatever you want to. You can either choose to live constructively or destructively; you can meet the future with pessimism or optimism. Do not forget that God, in His grace, gave you life – with a sublime purpose. Every day is a gift from the loving hand of God, and you can only live life to the full when you surrender to His purpose for your life. Achieving your purpose in life depends on your relationship with Him.

If life has a spiritual foundation, it must also have a spiritual goal. It is by acknowledging this truth and following it in your own life that you are guaranteed complete deliverance, joy, and fulfillment. Then you can utilize God's precious gift of life to the full.

A DIFFICULT TASK

And who is equal to such a task? (2 Corinthians 2:16)

At times, you will wrestle with difficult tasks that test your strength and skills to the limit. When you accepted Jesus Christ as the Lord of your life, you agreed to obey Him in all things. But now He may have called you to do something that you feel totally inadequate to handle.

Many followers of Christ become frustrated in their work for God because they try to do things in their own limited strength, instead of looking beyond themselves to the wisdom, power, and ability that God provides. God never calls you to do something that He knows you cannot do, even if you think it is beyond your ability. When God calls you to do something for Him, He supplies the skills needed.

When you face a difficult task, don't become intimidated by the degree of difficulty, but ask the Holy Spirit to give you the wisdom and insight you need to succeed.

Through the power of Jesus Christ, and the inspiration of the Holy Spirit, you will overcome discouragements and complete the task in a way that pleases Him.

A NEW APPROACH

He who was seated on the throne said, "I am making everything new!" (Revelation 21:5)

The heart of the gospel is that God entered human history in the Person of the living Christ. It is an awesome truth and a mystery that has us kneeling before the omnipotent God in worship and wonder.

The fact that Christ can identify with us, and us with Him, opens new horizons of greatness beyond our comprehension. Jesus Christ came to take you from failure and despair into a place where you could reach spiritual maturity. When this happens, your circumstances change radically and irreversibly. You are able to face your problems from a completely new perspective and with a new attitude.

Through the coming of Jesus Christ to our sin-wracked world, God came to reveal the mystery of His omnipotence and deity, so that even the most simple-hearted can understand it. This means that if you embrace Jesus as your Savior and Redeemer, your life will never be the same again. His coming will make "everything" in your life "new".

ALL THINGS
WORK FOR GOOD

*"For there is nothing hidden that will not be disclosed,
and nothing concealed that will not be known or
brought out into the open." (Luke 8:17)*

Dishonest people often become very wealthy, while honest people often struggle financially. People who deliberately harm their bodies sometimes seem to thrive, while health-conscious people sometimes contract all kinds of illnesses. The complaint continues to resound: good people suffer while the wicked prosper.

Before you join this woeful choir, remind yourself that life as we know it is not the end. What we experience now is passing and temporary, but the true life to which Christians aspire is eternal and lasting. Those who hold fast to their faith and persevere to the end will receive their just reward, not from people, but from God Himself.

Nothing that happens in this world is hidden from God. The most insignificant event is known to Him. We will all be called to give an account for our lives one day. So if it seems as if life is treating you badly, don't be discouraged or give up. Renew your trust in Jesus Christ and remember, "Be faithful, even to the point of death, and I will give you the crown of life" (Rev. 2:10).

DO SOMETHING WITH YOUR LIFE

But one thing I do: Forgetting what is behind and straining toward what is ahead, I press on toward the goal. (Philippians 3:13-14)

There are many elements within the human personality that compete for recognition and fulfillment. The complexity of human nature is emphasized by the fact that we fulfill diverse roles in our lives. As we move through different phases of life, we shift focus, often without being aware of it.

People who achieve success know the importance of specialization. They set themselves goals and strive to achieve them. Make sure that your goal is worthy of your very best. Some people strive for academic success while others focus on business or the arts. Whichever field you choose, if you are Christ's disciple you will want to make the world a better place.

The highest goal in your life is to conform more and more to the image of Christ. Christ calls you to the most noble way of life that you can live. He does not only call you but He equips you to reach heights that you would not have been able to reach in your own strength.

Let your life be meaningful and achieve your full potential through the power of the indwelling Christ.

ARE YOU A WORKAHOLIC?

In vain you rise early and stay up late,
toiling for food to eat – for He grants
sleep to those He loves. (Psalm 127:2)

Many people are addicted to their work. Whether they are involved in spiritual or secular work, they allow their work to control every area of their lives. Then they have little or no time for their families or leisure.

Whether their addiction is motivated by a desire for achievement, to establish security or to amass riches, the inevitable outcome is a breakdown of health, disintegration of family life, and a distorted view of life.

God expects Christians to perform their daily tasks with dedication and integrity, and to glorify Him in all things. However, He also expects you to spend time resting and relaxing, so that you can return to your job refreshed and strengthened and so reach your full potential.

This can only be achieved if you maintain a healthy balance between work and play. Remain sensitive to the voice of the Holy Spirit, then you will be able to give work and rest their rightful place in your daily routine, knowing that God will abundantly supply all your needs as you obey Him and structure your life according to His will.

WORD OF LIFE: GOD'S WORD

I want you to know, brothers, that the gospel I preached is not something that man made up. (Galatians 1:11)

No right-minded Christian would venture into life without the Word of God. From the beginning of time, people have developed theories on a wide variety of subjects. Some of these are based on religious convictions or philosophical premises; others are the product of imagination.

Many people are skeptical about the Bible. Others apply scientific principles to analyze the Bible in their quest for evidence that will placate their reason. This leads to conflicting views that do little more than confuse and obscure the issue of the authority of the Bible.

Although the Word of God has been fiercely criticized through the ages, it has remained steadfast. Theories are replaced and scientific premises changed, but the eternal Word of the eternal God, based on truth and wisdom from above, remains constant.

The Bible was divinely inspired. The Gospels establish a pattern for daily life that has stood the test of time. Abide steadfastly by the Bible's teachings. You will find them to be a source of never-ending inspiration, stability, and peace.

RESPECT THE SCRIPTURES

*All Scripture is God-breathed and is useful for
teaching, rebuking, correcting and training
in righteousness. (2 Timothy 3:16)*

The Bible is an essential life-manual for Christians. From it we draw guidance, admonition, hope, and everything necessary for spiritual development. It is, however, often abused, even by those who acknowledge it as the Word of God. This happens when verses are used out of context to construct religious theories that are inevitably divested of any true meaning.

For centuries people have tried to interpret the prophecies of the Scriptures to fit their own times, forgetting that the Lord expressly told His followers that it is not for us to know when these things are to happen. Many believe that we are now living in the "last days". But only God knows when the end will come. Never try to answer divine questions in human terms. You are not expected to strive to know about things that God keeps secret. Rather, you are expected to trust the Master to bring all things to their God-determined end.

The Bible encompasses the whole world, but it also speaks deeply to the individual soul. It is especially for the latter purpose that the Scriptures may be most useful to you.

THE LIVING WORD

Then He opened their minds so they could understand the Scriptures. (Luke 24:45)

There are many people who regard Bible study as a burdensome duty, and struggle through the prescribed daily passage. Others find that they don't understand what they are reading, or that their daily concerns take away their desire to read the Bible. Many people only read the Bible just before going to sleep, when they are tired and cannot possibly take in what they are reading.

If you are having problems with Bible study, it might be worthwhile to consider if perhaps you are spending more time reading *about* God than spending time *with* God.

It is necessary to know the Incarnate Word personally so that you can live the life of spiritual abundance that He offers you. In order to know Him, reach out to Him in the silence of your inner room through meditation and prayer. Then you can live out what you know by serving Him among your fellow men.

If you draw near to God in this manner, you will find that the Word starts to come alive with new meaning for you because you are no longer merely reading a book. Instead you are *living* the Word together with its Author!

THE SPIRIT GIVES INSIGHT

"But it is the Spirit in a man, the breath of the Almighty, that gives him understanding." (Job 32:8)

You read a stirring book, listen to delightful music, or see something in God's creation that leaves you speechless. You feel inspired, fulfilled, and uplifted. Such things not only provide a refuge for your spirit, but also give you insight into and a deeper knowledge of life.

But the greatest Source of insight and inspiration comes when you allow Christ into your life. Contrary to general belief, the insight that Christ brings is not restricted to spiritual matters, but encompasses and enriches every aspect of life.

When you accept that Christ lives in you and is at work in you, that He reveals Himself in and through you, your business, social, and cultural life will take on new dimensions and you will be full of new ideas. Your horizons will broaden and your insight deepen.

To be conscious of Christ's presence, you need to live with Him constantly and allow the Holy Spirit to guide you. As you cultivate this lifestyle, your life will pulsate with the insight and inspiration that the Spirit of God reveals to you.

JESUS CHRIST'S SIMPLICITY

Yet I am writing you a new command; its truth is seen in Him and you, because the darkness is passing and the true light is already shining. (1 John 2:8)

Religion has always been a controversial subject. Since the beginning of time people have argued about doctrinal issues and much blood has been shed in the name of the Prince of Peace. This is distressing and confusing to ordinary people whose only desire is to experience the reality and the abundance of Christ in their lives.

Too many Christians are fiercely dogmatic instead of being Christ-centered. They argue about details of doctrine and isolate themselves from their fellow Christians. Their love for Christ is not big enough to embrace those who differ from them theologically.

If you are experiencing spiritual confusion and feel inclined to abandon your faith, step back from all your doubts and uncertainties and look again at the holy simplicity of the living Savior.

Despite His greatness and uniqueness, Jesus lived a simple life. He was at home with all kinds of people and they were able to identify with Him. He made the tenets of religion understandable to everyone. He showed that the most important commandment is to love God and our neighbor. Let this be the motivating force in our lives.

LOVE IS THE ANSWER

And this is my prayer: that your love may abound more and more in knowledge and depth of insight, so that you may be able to discern what is best. (Philippians 1:9-10)

Decision-making is often very complex. The choice you make today may influence your future, finances, personal life, career and family. Whatever the circumstances, unless you remain level-headed, you run the risk of being overwhelmed by the anxiety of uncertainty, and your fear of the consequences.

You need the guidance and wisdom of the Holy Spirit to provide you with clarity of thought and vision. He has an eternal perspective, while you can only see the here and now. For this reason, and so that you can obtain peace of mind, it is essential to pray constantly for the guidance of the Holy Spirit.

To prepare yourself for this guidance, you need to develop an intimate, personal relationship with the living Christ, so that your thoughts can be focused on His will. The more you love Jesus, the closer you will live to Him, and the clearer you will hear Him speak to you through the promptings of His Holy Spirit.

Making definite decisions!

Elijah went before the people and said, "How long will you waver between two opinions? If the LORD is God, follow Him; but if Baal is God, follow him." (1 Kings 18:21)

Sometimes it is difficult to make a decision you feel completely comfortable with. You hesitate and waver between two options in the hope that someone else will make the decision for you.

Life gives its treasures to those who make positive and definite decisions. These people are not swayed to and fro by every new idea or set of circumstances. Once they have made a decision they do not change their minds.

The fear of making the wrong decision causes hesitancy, tension, and uncertainty. But it is better to make wrong decisions and learn from your failures than to live with indecision.

If you let God guide you, you have a Source of wisdom that becomes more powerful the more you use it. Consider every decision in prayer before God. Spend time with Him, consider alternatives, and open yourself to the guidance of His Holy Spirit. When you feel in your heart that you should move in a certain direction, go forward decisively, conscious of His indwelling presence. Then you will live with confidence.

GOD IS EVERYTHING

"What good will it be for a man if he gains the whole world, yet forfeits his soul? Or what can a man give in exchange for his soul?" (Matthew 16:26)

We dream about what we want to do, and our dreams determine the quality of our lives. You can idly dream and allow the years to pass without achieving anything worthwhile. Or your dreams can inspire you to take action and you can conquer the world.

The dream that inspires you should be big enough to pose a challenge. If your dreams limit you to gathering material possessions or living a frivolous social life, you are not living up to your potential. Remember that you were created in the image of God. God has destined you for greater things.

Cultivate a growing awareness of God's living presence in your life. It is possible that your fascination with the things of this world holds a greater attraction for you than the power and beauty of the living God. Material objects become of primary importance to you, and that which is important to God is set aside. It is only by deliberately turning to God and living according to His standards that you can determine the true value of life. Remember, without God you have nothing!

ADVICE FOR DIFFICULT TIMES

In all your ways acknowledge Him, and He will
make your paths straight. (Proverbs 3:6)

God wants to help you with your problems, and He is more than able to help you. This He makes abundantly clear in His infallible Word.

Life is full of problems. Some are undeserved and unexpected; others are the result of our own foolish behavior. Whatever the cause may be, if you do not find a solution, your problems begin to dominate your life.

If you have a problem for which you honestly and sincerely want a solution, lay it before your heavenly Father. Put Him first and relegate your problem to second place. Trust God with your problem. Affirm His sovereignty in your heart and mind and allow Him to create order from your confusion and bewilderment.

In His time and in His way He will answer your questions. There is no problem that He cannot solve. He cares for you and He can do far more than you are able to think or imagine. You will experience new spiritual strength because you have given God His rightful place in your life.

INTELLIGENT FOOL

"Watch out! Be on your guard against all kinds of greed; a man's life does not consist in the abundance of his possessions." (Luke 12:15)

A person can be intelligent yet lack wisdom. Others are less intellectually able, yet have much wisdom. Foolishness and wisdom have to do with the spirit of people and their relationship to God.

The man in the parable in Luke 12 had become rich through his careful planning and intelligence. He was hard-working, which is why he reaped abundant harvests. He was also ambitious.

Yet Jesus called him a fool because he neglected his soul. He was so busy accumulating wealth that he neglected God. Every person who ignores God is a fool.

He was especially foolish since he did not prepare for eternity. He could see as far as his old age but he did not have the insight to see beyond this world. And because he did not take God into account, he missed both his old age and eternity with Christ.

Make room for God on your life's agenda and in your planning, or you could labor in vain. Take eternity into account. Guard against the danger of being rich in earthly possessions yet poor before God.

DON'T BE MISLED

*See to it that no one takes you captive through hollow
and deceptive philosophy, which depends on human
tradition and the basic principles of this world
rather than on Christ. (Colossians 2:8)*

Some people can present their ideas and theories in
very convincing ways. This is especially true in spiritual matters, and even more so with the Christian
faith. Much unhappiness has been caused by such
people, who are both destructive and divisive. It is all
too easy to take a Scripture passage and to use it out
of context to support a particular theory. However,
the consequences can be far-reaching and disastrous.

Ask God for the wisdom to understand certain pas-
sages from the Scriptures, and also ask the guidance
of the Holy Spirit in assessing the theories and argu-
ments that other people force upon you in their quest
to get you to share their views.

Continually nurture an awareness of the presence
of the living Christ, who is with you at all times. In
this way you will remain sensitive to the promptings
of the Holy Spirit who will guide your thoughts and
deeds in His special way. However convincing others
may appear, unreservedly place yourself in the care
of Jesus Christ, and He will always make His will
known to you.

THE ART OF LIVING

"As a shepherd looks after his scattered flock when he is with them, so will I look after My sheep. I will rescue them from all the places where they were scattered on a day of clouds and darkness." (Ezekiel 34:12)

People often act like sheep. Just as sheep sometimes mindlessly follow one another, so people are inclined to follow the masses or public opinion. Just as sheep huddle together, so people look for comfort and protection from each other in times of crisis. And just as a sudden shock causes sheep to scatter, so people are driven apart by shock and confusion.

Many people will say it is impossible to change, but that is not true. You don't have to live with uncertainty or insecurity or nervous fear. This certainly is not the life that Jesus Christ offers you.

Through the Spirit of the living Christ, He is with you in every situation to protect you. He is omnipotent and all-knowing – a Father who watches over His children. He is always there, waiting for you to open the door of your life to Him, so that He can take over and lead you along His perfect way (Rev. 3:20). At all times stay in contact with the Master and you will be guaranteed a life of tranquility and peace of mind.

SENSITIVE TO GOD'S GUIDANCE

I will instruct you and teach you in the
way you should go. (Psalm 32:8)

It is not always easy to discern the will of God. Very few know exactly what God expects of them. Most people ask, "What is God's will for me in this situation?" Of course we know that God expects us to obey the Ten Commandments and to love as He commanded us to. But when it comes to the personal complexities of life we cannot always so easily see the will of God.

An intimate relationship with Jesus is necessary for you to know God's guidance so that you can do His will. Then you become sensitive to His ways. Every time you act contrary to His will, your heart feels uneasy.

As you study the Word you will learn to know God's will. A practical knowledge of the Scriptures makes it much easier to know and understand God's principles as they apply to you.

Living in fellowship with Christ and obeying His Word assures you of His guidance through the Holy Spirit. Then your words and deeds are brought into line with God's will for you.

WHAT IS THE PURPOSE OF LIFE?

"My food," said Jesus, "is to do the will of Him who sent Me and to finish His work." (John 4:34)

Does life have a purpose or is it a meaningless struggle from birth to death? Is it necessary to have a goal? Some people set themselves goals that demand all their energy and concentration. They look forward to reveling in a position of authority over others. Others, who are more broad-minded, see success as service to their fellow man.

People all over the world believe that achieving their particular goals will bring them the happiness and satisfaction they desire.

As a dedicated and committed Christian your highest goal should be to please God – and not yourself. This is the key to a purposeful and satisfying life. There is no greater goal in life than to do the will of God. That is why you were born, and deviating from it leads only to frustration and dissatisfaction.

Living to carry out God's will requires a high level of commitment. But it brings joy untold because it brings you in touch with the Source of joy and fills your life with riches and blessings that are the inheritance of those who love and serve Christ.

TO KNOW THE WILL OF GOD

May the God of peace ... equip you with everything good for doing His will. (Hebrews 13:20-21)

There are guidelines that apply generally to all Christians wanting to find the will of God. The call to sanctification, to spiritual growth, to love and serve your fellow man, are just a few. But there comes a time when the issue becomes personal and you need to ask, "Lord, what do You want of *me*?" If God has a specific task for you, He will guide you to fulfill it. As you seek His guidance, you will feel enthusiastic about the things He is calling you to do.

This enthusiasm is important as it will help you to discern the will of God. You will be inspired by new, creative ideas and methods for effective service that will unexpectedly fill your thoughts. Keep your thoughts open and your spirit receptive to the work of God's Holy Spirit. Allow Him to increase or diminish your enthusiasm so that you can determine your path through life.

Seeking the will of God through prayer has the additional benefit of a more intimate relationship with the Lord. It means that you will keep your spiritual ear tuned to the voice of God.

WHERE ARE YOU GOING?

But thanks be to God, who always leads us in triumphal procession in Christ. (2 Corinthians 2:14)

Some people seem to succeed with little effort, while others are hounded by defeat. Nothing happens by chance – at least not in the lives of God's children. Nobody is successful by accident, nor is anybody a failure by chance.

Every person chooses what they want to be and where they want to go. It is not always easy to choose which road to follow. And this is where accepting Christ as Lord of your life puts divine powers into action. Your values are set in right order and they supply you with an inspired yet practical goal.

Choosing your goal with Christ's guidance is the highest form of common sense. Such cooperation with God will result in tremendous blessing in your life.

Choosing your goals with Christ's help ensures that you can live with a clear conscience. It will bring joy, confidence, and enthusiasm into your life. Striving to reach your goal then becomes just as joyful as its attainment. If you walk the path of life in the light of God, the whole journey becomes a joyous experience.

A GRACIOUS SIGNPOST

Who, then, is the man that fears the LORD? He will instruct him in the way chosen for him. He will spend his days in prosperity. (Psalm 25:12-13)

Our lives can become extremely complicated. Many people find themselves lost in a maze and cannot see a way out. They are forced to make hasty decisions that influence them and their loved ones. Many cannot handle such situations and are tossed hither and thither like driftwood across the sea of life. Their lives are controlled by the storms, the tides, and the winds and, to their great relief, sometimes the calm.

But God will accompany you along the path He has ordained for you, if you follow Him obediently. Initially it may seem as if the things that happen are not in your best interests, but when you consider the end result, you will realize that God's way is the best for you under all circumstances.

Lay every decision that you have to make, whether big or small, before Jesus Christ in prayer. Share your life with the living Christ in the sure knowledge that He, the Son of the omniscient God, will guide you along a safe path.

OUR PROMISE

I will counsel you and watch over you. (Psalm 32:8)

The psalmist is so joyful about God's forgiveness and all-embracing love that he wants to tell others about it. He pleads: "Do not be like the horse or the mule, which have no understanding but must be controlled by bit and bridle or they will not come to you. Many are the woes of the wicked, but the LORD's unfailing love surrounds the man who trusts in Him" (Ps. 32:9-10).

What a comforting and blessed promise! It encourages us when we are uncertain about the road ahead. Many people give us advice and recommend some course of action. Often it is useful and professional advice, but we are unsure whether it is really applicable to us.

We have a Friend who promised to be our Counselor. He always watches over us for our good. He knows the road from beginning to end and He knows what is best for us. Let us ask His guidance from day to day, and believe without a doubt that He will advise us and that He will watch over us.

OCTOBER

DISCIPLESHIP

GOD CHOOSES HIS WORKERS

Being confident of this, that He who began a good work in you will carry it on to completion until the day of Christ Jesus. (Philippians 1:6)

In every generation, followers of God have proclaimed His truth and done His will. Some have been highly esteemed but others remained unknown. All of them, famous and unknown, loved God with a fervor that inspired and challenged their fellow men.

Paul never forgot his meeting with the Master on the road to Damascus; Brother Lawrence met Christ in his kitchen; John Wesley felt his heart strangely warmed in a room in Aldersgate Street.

The Lord comes to each of us in a personal and unique way to meet us where we are. We do not all have a Damascus Road experience, because the Savior prepares a special experience that is uniquely suited to our individuality.

As your experience of Jesus deepens and expands into constructive service, you will become aware of a divine plan unfolding in your life. This plan may not be particularly dramatic or impressive by the standards of the world, but it will be God's plan for your life. In accomplishing it you will experience immense joy and profound satisfaction.

DISCIPLES AND DISCIPLINE

Therefore, if anyone is in Christ, he is a new creation. (2 Corinthians 5:17)

Some people want a religion that suits their personal lifestyle. They seek a church that places few demands on them. Unfortunately, they never experience the power of a living faith.

If the challenge to discipleship is to be truly effective, it must influence every facet of your life. You will have to admit your weaknesses, confess the sins and failures of your past, and recognize your dependency on God.

If you feel you can't live up to the standards of the Lord, and it seems as if your spiritual life is falling apart, share your unhappy circumstances with God and ask for His help. No one has ever asked Jesus for help in vain.

When you accept Christ's assistance, you accept the responsibility of discipleship and discipline. Your mind and spirit should be brought under the dominion of the Holy Spirit. In this way your thoughts become constructive and your character strong so that you can do the will of God and become a disciple who is worthy of your calling.

USE GOD'S GIFTS

*I want you to stress these things, so that those who have
trusted in God may be careful to devote themselves
to doing what is good. (Titus 3:8)*

Every disciple should strive for an ever deeper experience of God's love as revealed through Jesus Christ. Even though you love Him deeply and know that He loves you, you yearn for the relationship to grow deeper. You know that prayer, Scripture-reading, meditation, and other spiritual disciplines enable you to grow in love, and the practical application of these principles must not be underestimated or ignored.

Many of Christ's disciples long for a more powerful faith but they do not use the faith they already have. Use the faith you have and you will find it becomes a working force in your everyday life.

The disciple who fully accepts his responsibility continually desires a more meaningful prayer life. He may ask God to grant him this beautiful gift, but he already has it. The way to God has been opened by Jesus Christ, and it is the privilege of the disciple to regularly walk upon this path with a firm step. God has already given you the roadmap for prayer – all you have to do is to use and develop it.

Exam time!

Then He said to him, "Follow Me!" (John 21:19)

For three exciting years Peter had been taught by the greatest Teacher ever. He had learned to become a dedicated disciple of Christ. And every now and again he had to take a test.

He failed geography, because the "rock" crumbled. He failed seamanship, because he sank beneath the waves through unbelief. He failed agriculture, because he could not distinguish between wheat and chaff, and so landed in Satan's hands. He failed human relations, because he denied His best Friend.

But, praise God, Christ does not call those who are able. He enables those whom He calls. Peter passed the test of faithfulness because when everybody else wanted to desert Jesus, Peter asked, "Where else can we go?" He passed the difficult test of faith with his testimony, "You are the Christ, the Son of the living God."

Now the final test is given and only one question appears on the page, "Simon, son of John, do you really love Me?" He passed the test of Christian discipleship with flying colors, and was ready to obey when Christ commanded, "Follow Me."

To do God's will according to God's way

*Teach me, O LORD, to follow Your decrees; then
I will keep them to the end. (Psalm 119:33)*

Many servants of the Lord diligently serve Him,
but do not truly love Him. They serve Him in many
different ways, but often these are ways of their own
choosing. When they are challenged to service that
demands sacrifice, they merely work harder at their
own choice.

While all work done for the Lord is good – no one
can work for the Lord without being blessed – the
only work that is truly beneficial is that done according to His holy will.

It is important to personally know the will of God
for yourself. If you have compassion for others' physical and spiritual needs, you will understand God's
will better. When the suffering of others compels you
to compassionate action, you are fulfilling the will of
the Lord.

Christ was always profoundly touched by people's
suffering, especially the suffering of the innocent. If
you become aware of someone's distress and you
offer your heart, soul, mind, and strength to God,
asking Him to enable you to help, you will be amazed
at the way God uses you in His service.

THE JOY OF OBEDIENCE

Moses did as the LORD commanded him. He took Joshua and had him stand before Eleazar the priest and the whole assembly. Then he laid his hands on him and commissioned him. (Numbers 27:22-23)

Faith and obedience are essential for Christian maturity and fulfillment. When Christians complain that they have lost the spark that used to bring them so much joy, they are probably trying to live in their own strength or do things their own way. When you do not place your trust in God or obey His will for your life, you are on course for a miserable spiritual existence and a meaningless life.

Moses stands out as a man who placed his faith in God despite opposition from the Egyptians and the Israelites. He obeyed the Word of God and was instrumental in the establishment of the nation of Israel, acting as mediator between the Israelites and God.

You too have an important role to play in life. You must guide others toward a deeper and more meaningful relationship with the living Christ. The only way in which you can hope to achieve success is to trust that He will give you the ability to accomplish your goal, and to obey His will unconditionally.

CHOOSE GOD'S WAY

Surely the arm of the LORD is not too short to save,
nor His ear too dull to hear. (Isaiah 59:1)

We often live as if God does not exist. We make our own plans and work hard to accomplish them. We develop ambitions and devise ventures without any thought of what God expects of us.

And, when we decide to follow our own way instead of God's way, things usually start going awry. We run into the proverbial brick wall and start thinking that bad luck is hounding us. We become despondent and feel that it is useless to attempt anything, because it will fail anyway.

The truth of the matter is that our problem is not bad luck, but our deliberate disobedience to God's call to live a nobler life. If things seem to be going wrong for you all the time, pause and consider why they are going awry. Are you choosing your own way instead of God's way?

However desperate your circumstances may be, things can turn around if you abandon your selfish ways and choose God's perfect way. Being obedient to God and walking in His way will bring deliverance from even the most wretched circumstances.

GOD WORKS THROUGH YOU

"Remain in Me, and I will remain in you. No branch can bear fruit by itself; it must remain in the vine. Neither can you bear fruit unless you remain in Me." (John 15:4)

You worship a miracle-working God whom you can call on in times of stress and tension. God will always give you what you need, because He is the Giver of every perfect gift and you are the blessed receiver.

Most people respond to the benevolence of God by trying to find some good deed they can do that will please Him. When you think of something, you do it enthusiastically and energetically. But are you sure this is what He wants you to do?

Discovering God's will for your life can be an exciting adventure. You may start out in various directions before you finally discover the path that He has set for you. But when you know that you are in His holy will, you will discover that you are no longer working *for* Him, but that He is working *through* you.

Then the road ahead opens up miraculously. Problems suddenly become opportunities and your faith becomes practical, alive, and dynamic. By working with God, you become an effective instrument in His hand.

WHAT ARE YOU LIVING FOR?

*To know this love that surpasses knowledge –
that you may be filled to the measure of all
the fullness of God. (Ephesians 3:19)*

Many people find life a monotonous routine without meaning or purpose. Day by day they go through the motions, always wondering what the meaning of life is. Others are ambitious and do all they can to come out ahead of the pack. But in their wild scramble to obtain worldly honors, they often sacrifice precious time and integrity.

Every person sooner or later starts seeking the true meaning of life. When monotony dulls your spirit and luxury leaves your soul sated, or when the ladder of success collapses, you ask, "What is the purpose of my life?"

The most meaningful reply has a spiritual basis. Nobody who has a vibrant relationship with the living Christ needs to ask this question; they are too busy living an abundant life through the power of Christ.

The glorious truth is that we are born to glorify God, to worship and serve Him.

Monotony, frustration and a sense of futility vanish when your life is committed unconditionally to His love.

WHO AM I?

Yet to all who received Him, to those who believed in His name, He gave the right to become children of God. (John 1:12)

We all have days when everything looks bare and dismal. We question the purpose of life by asking, "Who am I really?"

In times of depression it is not uncommon for people to question their identity as well as the purpose of life. This confusion could arise from a change in lifestyle or the workplace, deep disappointment, illness, death, and any of a number of factors that shake your stability and tranquility and cause you to sink into a well of helplessness and hopelessness.

If you find yourself questioning your identity and the purpose of your existence, remember the glorious heritage that you have received through the grace of God. Through your faith in Jesus Christ, and by embracing Him as your Savior and Redeemer, your life will find new meaning and purpose.

He offers you the greatest of all privileges and the only true life when you, by identifying with the living Christ, become a child of God. Life can have no greater meaning than that.

CHOSEN TO BEAR FRUIT

"I chose you and appointed you to go and bear fruit –
fruit that will last." (John 15:16)

God's people are new creations. This is the result of a personal experience with the living Christ, which we enter into because of God's love for us. His love is pure undeserved mercy and grace. Through His grace and our surrender to His love, we become fruit-bearing disciples.

God called us to serve Him with joy, no matter how hard the task. If we do not have joy, our service becomes nothing more than slave labor. Our life should radiate joy, because God gave us the privilege of being His children and working for Him.

We were chosen to serve in love. Without love, we cannot be ambassadors of the Source of all true love. Love gives us a passion for souls and keeps us from competing with one another for petty honors.

Since Christ calls us His friends, we must guard against becoming like the elder brother in the parable of the prodigal son who begrudged serving his father. We are fellow-workers with Christ and our service and the fruit we bear should be evidence of all that is best and most noble in our lives.

REVIVAL STARTS IN MY HEART

"But seek first His kingdom and His righteousness, and all these things will be given to you as well." (Matthew 6:33)

Some people believe that their convictions and doctrines are the solution to every sickness and disease that besets society. They forget that imperfection is part of our sinful nature and that we are living in a world torn apart by sin.

It is impossible to create a new world without new people. It is futile to try to reform others if your relationship with God is not right. The best place to start healing this world is within yourself. Kneel down and fervently ask God to start a revival within you.

When you live in harmony with God, it is possible to really influence others because, as Jesus said, "The kingdom of God is within you" (Luke 17:21).

We have to become aware of God's kingdom first and allow it to govern our lives. Then it will be revealed in our characters, attitudes, and deeds and cause ripples that will touch others. Jesus will enable you to positively influence that part of His vineyard where He placed you to represent His kingdom.

THE COST OF DISCIPLESHIP

"If anyone would come after Me, he must deny himself and take up his cross daily and follow Me." (Luke 9:23)

Let today's Scripture verse prompt us to prayerfully examine ourselves, bearing in mind Christ's sacrifice and love. "Self-denial" is not a word that falls easily on the ears of sinners. Hearing about "taking up the cross" is definitely not music to our ears. But we are called to do so because Jesus made the incomparable sacrifice to redeem us.

Jesus sacrificed His life for us on the cross. His sacrifice was complete and total, because He gave His all for humankind.

Consider His unfathomable love that compelled Him to make this sacrifice. Then you will realize that you and all of humanity owe the Redeemer infinitely more than we could ever give.

Only absolute surrender to Jesus Christ can, in a minor way, be compared to His sacrifice. This calls us to a life of relinquishment, cross-bearing and self-denial for every one who calls himself a Christian.

THE ULTIMATE GOAL IN LIFE

*We who are alive are always being given over to death
for Jesus' sake, so that His life may be revealed
in our mortal body. (2 Corinthians 4:11)*

Some people have a hidden agenda for doing good deeds. There are also many people whose dedicated service to others is inspired by their commitment to Jesus Christ, and humankind is enriched by such people.

Regardless of how you express your Christian faith, never forget that service can only be the expression of a sincere relationship with Jesus Christ. As a Christian you are not only called to do good works, but also to reflect the life of Christ in your thoughts and deeds – even though it may be in a very small measure.

Christ calls His disciples to share their lives with Him. This wonderful fellowship and intimacy are the Master's gift to those disciples who love Him and have committed their lives to Him.

If Christlikeness is the goal of your life, you will develop a much better understanding of the needs of your fellow man. Commit yourself to becoming Christlike and people will see Him in your service to them.

REMEMBER WHO YOU ARE

But you are a chosen people, a royal priesthood, a holy
nation, a people belonging to God, that you may declare
the praises of Him who called you out of darkness
into His wonderful light. (1 Peter 2:9)

Do you sometimes feel unsure of your faith and go through times of doubt and depression? You are tempted to give up trying to be a Christian or fellowshiping with Christ's followers.

Remember that there are two distinctly discernible sides to your Christian life: God's side and yours. God called you to live in harmony with Him. You responded and became His disciple. This is reason enough for you to stand strong in your faith and to live the spiritual life with confidence and courage.

You belong to the living Savior: He bought you with His blood and accepted you as His own. Remember your rich inheritance and the kind of life God has called you to. Nothing can be a substitute for the right relationship with your heavenly Father. This world might offer seemingly attractive temptations that are more appealing than what Christ offers you.

You have been "chosen"; you belong to a "royal priesthood" and you have been "set apart". Muster all the strength you possess to be true to this high and lofty calling.

WHO? ME?

"Who am I, that I should go to Pharaoh and bring the Israelites out of Egypt?" (Exodus 3:11)

People have often been challenged to undertake tasks for which they thought they were ill-equipped.

Unfortunately many people have allowed great opportunities to slip through their fingers, merely because they convinced themselves that they were inadequate for the task. They feebly excused themselves, declaring they were not qualified for the situation facing them.

Some of the greatest people in history had no qualifications for the task they undertook. They simply took the opportunities God gave and carried out the task in His strength.

Possibly you are facing such a challenge at this very moment. Perhaps you doubt your own ability to see it through. Take your problem to God in prayer and if it is His will that you should act, do so in complete dependence on Him and with the conviction that Christ would not call you to a task for which He does not equip you.

STRENGTH LIES
IN SMALL THINGS

*"Your beginnings will seem humble,
so prosperous will your future be."* (Job 8:7)

Many people are so excited by important things in life that they fail to notice the apparently unimportant matters that carry the seeds of true greatness. Many industrial and business ventures originated in a back-yard or a simple kitchen. They all started with an idea backed by knowledge, and were made possible through hard work and an iron will to succeed.

There are people who hide behind the false belief that everything worthwhile has already been thought of by somebody else, and that it is therefore not worth the trouble to start something new. Nothing could be further from the truth. The world is full of ideas that are waiting to be developed.

True Christianity is applicable to every facet of life, and if it is to be effective it must encompass your entire life.

True Christianity can never be confined to the inside of the church. All constructive ideas have their origins in God, the great Creator. Those who wait on Him in an attitude of excited anticipation, who are sensitive to His guidance, will be open to new ideas.

ABSOLUTE COMMITMENT

But whatever was to my profit I now consider
loss for the sake of Christ. (Philippians 3:7)

Often people set out on their walk with Christ with
great commitment and enthusiasm. After an intense
spiritual experience, they are on an emotional high.
However, this mountaintop experience does not last
very long. As soon as the initial enthusiasm starts to
wane, many people return to their old life, habits, and
ways.

Never forget that Christ, for your salvation, gave
up everything – even His life! Nothing was more
important to Him than His mission to save souls for
God. He wanted to lead people from the darkness of
sin and misery into the glorious light of God. In order
to achieve this, He put all personal desires aside, for-
sook all comfort and security, and, for your sake and
mine, sacrificed His life!

Your greatest desire should be to live your life according to the will of the One who sacrificed His life
for you. Commitment and dedication involve searching for God's will and remaining true to it. It requires
putting aside your own preferences and desires and
opening up your heart to the influence of the Holy
Spirit.

GOD GRANTS SELF-CONFIDENCE

It is better to take refuge in the LORD
than to trust in man. (Psalm 118:8)

Many of God's children lack self-confidence. They believe in God and in His goodness and grace, yet they enter each day with fear and trepidation. They are convinced that others are better than they are and that others don't think much of them. They try to walk along life's path as unobtrusively as possible.

If you have had a real and living encounter with Christ, you will no longer suffer from an inferiority complex because you will forget about yourself. If you accept Him as the Lord of your life and make up your mind to serve Him and obey Him in everything, you will stop thinking about the opinions of others.

You develop a more Christlike view of life when you accept His invitation to abide in Him (see John 15:1-8). What others think or say is then of no concern to you. Christ has given you a new perspective and you face each day with confidence. Your only desire is to please Him and not men.

Forget about yourself, live for Christ and your inferiority will be something of the past.

Fragile containers

*But we have this treasure in jars of clay to
show that this all-surpassing power is from
God and not from us. (2 Corinthians 4:7)*

Kings of old used to store their treasures in clay pots.
In the same way that a tattered book can contain lofty
thoughts, these plain earthen pots became the containers of precious treasures.

This is exactly what it is like in the kingdom of
God. Paul compares our lives to earthen vessels in
which we carry the glorious message of the Gospel
of Christ.

The earthen vessel is an image of human frailty
and mortality, but it is also an image of the Potter's
ability to re-create our lives.

When He calls us to be His disciples, we shrink
back because we are aware of our imperfection and
inadequacy – but God does not necessarily call those
who are able; He enables those whom He calls.

We should always be in awe at the realization that
God uses us – sinful as we are – to carry His treasures!
We should never draw attention to ourselves instead
of focusing it on God's treasures. The glory always
belongs to God.

IN HIS MAJESTY'S SERVICE

*Therefore I glory in Christ Jesus in
my service to God. (Romans 15:17)*

Many church members complain that there are very
few willing hands to do the work necessary in the
congregation. There is much to be done but there are
very few willing to do it.

There are two things to remember when you begin
serving. The first is that you are serving the living
God and not people. You are working for His glory
and honor. The second is that God will never call you
into His service without equipping you with the ability to do that specific task.

To offer to serve Jesus among His people is both an
indescribable privilege and your Christian duty. You
have the gracious honor of reflecting the love of God.
If there is any doubt with regard to your ability, then
seek the help of the Holy Spirit. If you remain open
to His guidance, He will inspire you with the power
of the living Christ and will enable you to faithfully
fulfill the task that He has called you to.

Offer yourself and your talents to Him and experience the joy of fulfillment.

PRIVILEGES AND RESPONSIBILITIES

So that Christ may dwell in your hearts through faith. (Ephesians 3:17)

There is no substitute for a personal relationship with the living Christ. Doctrines and creeds are necessary to clarify our understanding and rituals can help to bring us into the right frame of mind for meeting with God. Unfortunately many people emphasize these side issues and forget that they are simply guidelines to bring us into the presence of the risen Savior.

The committed Christian should not dissociate himself from the world in order to know Christ intimately. To isolate yourself from others because they do not share the same spiritual experience is spiritual arrogance. This does not reflect the example Jesus Christ set when He lived on earth.

You have specific responsibilities and privileges because Christ lives in you. You are called to reflect the glory of Christ. It is sobering to think that non-Christians form an impression of Christ by the way you behave in situations that they also face.

Christ knows everything about you. He supplements your imperfection with His complete perfection; your weakness He strengthens with His power; your lack of love He ignites with His perfect love.

SERVANTHOOD

After that, He poured water into a basin and began to wash His disciples' feet, drying them with the towel that was wrapped around Him. (John 13:5)

Much has been written about love and humility. Many have tried to explain the true meaning of their application in life. Despite all the profound statements, the world still has a desperate need for the demonstration of true love and humility, so that the wounds of this world may be healed.

Everywhere we turn we are faced with examples of behavior that is in direct contradiction with everything that God expects of His people.

Jesus provided us with a practical demonstration of what God requires. On the eve of His crucifixion, He took the role of servant by humbly washing His disciples' feet. He proved that humility can be exalted and that love can conquer all things.

There is a great need to let the humility and love of Jesus conquer pride and hatred throughout the world. Humility and love are the only paths to lasting relationships. For this, Christ died on the cross. Let us, therefore, become servants for Christ.

PROVE THAT
YOU LOVE GOD

*But if anyone obeys His word, God's love is
truly made complete in him. (1 John 2:5)*

There is often a sentimentality in our spiritual life that undermines the Christian faith. To counteract this, many Christians advocate an unemotional faith that is often also aggressive.

Telling God how much you love Him may seem sentimental, yet it is one of the most inspiring things you can do. It fortifies your heart, focuses your thoughts on eternal realities, and confirms the convictions that you have always held but seldom expressed.

To tell God you love Him entails much more than a fleeting sentiment, because love without action is useless. Love requires uplifting and inspirational deeds. James asks, "What good is it if a man claims to have faith but has no deeds?" (James 2:14). How genuine can your love for God truly be if you are aware of a serious need and do nothing to alleviate it?

When you unreservedly tell God that you love Him, you offer your best to Him and express your willingness to serve Him wherever He wishes to use you. Love that does not manifest itself practically becomes a gimmick that lacks dynamic spirituality.

IN THE SERVICE OF GOD

Do your best to present yourself to God as one approved, a workman who does not need to be ashamed and who correctly handles the word of truth. (2 Timothy 2:15)

God has many workers who are active in His service. They attend church meetings, do good deeds, and seldom have idle time.

You can become so involved in God's work that you lose sight of what God wants you to do. You diligently work *for* God without working *with* Him. You may be frantically busy and other Christians may be impressed with what you are doing. You may even delude yourself into thinking that you are doing extremely important work. And then one day, something dries up in your soul, you become tense, and you snap. You cease your Christian activities because of a nervous breakdown, and a life that may have done great things for God is lost.

The most important duty of any Christian worker is to strengthen his relationship with God every day. If you are too busy to spend time with Him in daily prayer, you cannot be an effective servant for Him.

CHOSEN BY GOD

"You did not choose Me, but I chose you." (John 15:16)

Many people date the beginning of their Christian walk to when they acknowledged the sovereignty of Christ in their lives. But their Christian experience actually began when the Holy Spirit started working in their imperfect lives. Perhaps they were antagonistic toward Christianity, yet were inexplicably restless and nothing could give them the satisfaction they yearned for.

The revelation of God's voice calling you – the fact that He chose you to serve Him – is often accompanied by inner conflict and confusion because you are not immediately willing to do what God is asking of you. Once you commit yourself to God, this inner struggle can be the beginning of a glorious spiritual ministry – as you open your life to the inflowing of the Holy Spirit.

You were chosen by God to serve Him and to live to the honor and glory of His Name. Those people who surrender unconditionally to the Lord when they hear Him calling, discover that their lives gain new meaning and purpose. What greater grace could be shown to an insignificant human being?

A LIFE OF FULFILLMENT

*For now we really live, since you are standing
firm in the Lord. (1 Thessalonians 3:8)*

Knowing that your service for Christ is effective is
a source of great joy. It may be something you said;
a kind deed; support in times of need; a sympathetic ear. The fact that the Master used you to draw
someone closer to Him leaves you feeling humbled,
awe-inspired and fulfilled.

Christ inspires people through His Holy Spirit to
be His witnesses, to proclaim the gospel, and to win
souls for God. This is the role God expects you to fulfill because you bear His holy Name.

True discipleship is never easy and you will have
to overcome many obstacles along the way. You will
taste disappointment and face adversity. In spite of
all this, never give up hope, but persevere in your
service as your Master did.

Seek the Lord in prayer and open your heart to
the Holy Spirit so that Christ can become an essential
part of your life. As He leads you along His path, you
will experience unparalleled fulfillment that can only
be found in serving Jesus Christ.

HOW CAN I SERVE GOD?

Your love has given me great joy and encouragement, because you, brother, have refreshed the hearts of the saints. (Philemon verse 7)

Many people fervently desire to serve the Lord, but they do not know how. As a result they experience a vacuum in their spiritual life. They become frustrated and complain that they remain unfulfilled. In their disappointment, they withdraw more and more, until they, in their opinion, wave a lost cause goodbye.

Every disciple of Jesus has a capacity for love. The most effective way to serve the Master is to share His love with others. Love can comfort, save the lost, and offer hope to those who need it. It can break down barriers, build bridges, establish relationships, and heal wounds.

If you are sincerely looking for a way to serve the Lord, why don't you start by loving others in His name. A telephone call, a letter, or a visit to somebody who is in distress will provide unprecedented joy and comfort.

Even more importantly, serving the Lord will bring a sense of fulfillment and satisfaction to your life.

PUT CHRIST FIRST IN YOUR LIFE

I want to know Christ and the power of His resurrection and the fellowship of sharing in His sufferings. (Philippians 3:10)

Many of God's servants are so busy working for Him, that they do not have regular quiet time. Few people will say, "I work for the Lord, therefore I do not have to pray." Rather, they are so active for the kingdom that their activities gradually become more important than their time with the Father. They are active for God without experiencing the presence and power of the living Christ.

Attempting to serve the Lord without the strength of the Holy Spirit results in frustration and ultimate disaster.

If your vision of Him grows dim, your service will become powerless and ineffective. This will happen if your spiritual reserves are not regularly replenished through prayer and meditation.

No matter how you serve the Master, you must put Him first in all your activities. Your service *for* Him must be the result of your intimate knowledge *of* Him. Only when He enjoys priority in all things, can you understand life from His perspective. Putting Christ first in your life and work makes you a more capable servant of God.

LOST OPPORTUNITIES

*"If you, even you, had only known on this day
what would bring you peace – but now it is
hidden from your eyes." (Luke 19:42)*

Few people can honestly say that they have no remorse about lost opportunities for doing a kind deed
or speaking an encouraging word. Every day offers
opportunities of cheering someone who is depressed,
helping someone going through deep waters, or
of speaking a friendly word to someone who feels
overwhelmed.

To be sensitive to the needs of others and to do all
you can to relieve their distress will prevent regrets.
It is impossible to enrich other people's lives through
love and kindness without simultaneously enriching
your own life. Giving yourself in love and service to
others is the privilege of all those who love Christ and
serve Him with sincere hearts.

Find God's purpose for your life as you serve
others in His glorious name. Do not brood over lost
opportunities. Make a definite decision to do better
today and tomorrow. Throw yourself enthusiastically
into serving others because of your exuberant joy
about God's goodness to you. Use every opportunity
in His strength, and the future will be free of any self-
reproach for you.

THE CRUCIAL POWER OF LOVE

"You have let go of the commands of God and are holding on to the traditions of men." (Mark 7:8)

Rituals and traditions have always played an important role in society. This is especially true in the church, where congregational life and practices are largely controlled by the church ordinances and liturgy.

While it is essential that any group of people must adhere to rules so that everything can run smoothly, it is of the utmost importance that these do not become the dominant factor in any Christian community.

The foundation of any denomination must be absolute surrender, devotion, and obedience to God, rising from pure love for Him. Jesus Christ must be central in all things and His will must take precedence over the will of people, regardless of how well meaning the latter may be.

To be a channel of the love of God, surrender yourself unconditionally to the guidance of the Holy Spirit. Then you will also be able to identify man-made rules with the wisdom of the Holy Spirit and to implement them in the love of God. In this way, you will be able to serve your community according to God's will, and in love.

NOVEMBER

CHRISTLIKENESS

CHRISTIANS ARE DIFFERENT

Therefore, as God's chosen people, holy and dearly loved, clothe yourselves with compassion, kindness, humility, gentleness and patience. (Colossians 3:12)

Because you are a Christian, people expect you to behave honorably. This is a challenging thought because it calls you to be Christlike. It is also a sobering thought because you realize that you constantly fail to live up to the standards Christ has set for His followers.

Your value system is determined by the Lord; your code of conduct honors others above yourself; you are called to be slow to judge and quick to forgive. When you are confronted with antagonism, you have the ability to demonstrate love in the face of hatred. Because you are a disciple of Jesus Christ, His Spirit is in you and He makes you different.

If this truth overwhelms you and causes you to feel inadequate, thank God that His Word gives you this guarantee, "My grace is sufficient for you, for My power is made perfect in weakness" (2 Cor. 12:9). It is precisely your inadequacy that can be transformed into constructive purposefulness if you relinquish it to the Master. As a Christian you possess something very special because the Spirit of Christ lives in you.

CHRISTLIKENESS-CHALLENGE

*Your attitude should be the same as that
of Christ Jesus. (Philippians 2:5)*

Different denominations depict Christianity according to their specific interpretations of His message, making it extremely difficult to understand what Christ's challenges to His followers really entail. However, one thing we know, those who call themselves Christians and walk in fellowship with Him must grow in the knowledge and grace of their Lord and Master so that they can become like Him.

To walk in fellowship with the living Christ, and grow in grace and the knowledge of Him requires spiritual discipline. You do not need to be a brilliant student, but you must use your mind to the best of your ability and serve your Master faithfully. As you do so, your thoughts will be free of fear, bitterness, hate, greed, pride, and other destructive forces.

If you feel inadequate to implement these high standards, recall all the wonderful promises of the Scriptures. The Bible encourages disciples to develop and maintain Jesus' attitude toward life.

Study how Jesus approached different people and partake of His wisdom in human relations. Willingly and unconditionally follow His guidance.

ONE WITH CHRIST

"Remain in Me, and I will remain in you." (John 15:4)

The central truth of the Christian message is that Christ lives in those who believe in Him. He was crucified, died and rose again, and He lives forever in the hearts and lives of those who love Him. Their greatest desire is to grow into the likeness of His image.

The realization that Christ lives in your spirit could be a highly emotional experience. But when the emotional fervor has cooled off, what remains in your daily life? Is His Spirit revealed in the sincerity of your motives, honesty of your objectives, unselfishness in your conduct, and love in your actions? To speak of Christ living in you while refusing to allow Him to find expression through your life, is nothing but a caricature of the Christian experience.

It is both a humbling and challenging thought that Christians are the only channel through which Christ can reveal Himself to this generation. The indwelling Spirit, however, overcomes our human weaknesses. He meets our human inadequacy by strengthening us. We simply have to draw from the strength Christ puts at our disposal.

CHRISTLIKENESS NEEDS GROWTH

*Instead, speaking the truth in love, we will in all
things grow up into Him who is the Head,
that is, Christ. (Ephesians 4:15)*

The moment you embraced Christ as your Savior and Redeemer, you accepted certain responsibilities. When you become a Christian, you start a new life with new values and fresh objectives. You no longer live to please yourself, but to please God. The greatest purpose in your life will be to serve others. The good deeds that you do for others are a practical expression of your faith.

New life in Christ requires certain things of you that you must honor if your spiritual strength is to be developed and maintained. As a Christian disciple, you have a solemn obligation to revere your Master and the goal of your life must be to glorify and please Him. You no longer live for your own pleasure. You must be totally obedient to the will of God, as it has been revealed to you in His Word. You must confess your sins to God and to those against whom you have transgressed.

Paul teaches that Christians must be filled with the fullness of God. Every Christian who loves his Lord is compelled to grow into Christ.

THE TRUE TEST OF DISCIPLESHIP

"By this all men will know that you are My disciples, if you love one another." (John 13:35)

Christ makes many demands on His disciples. How we respond to these demands distinguishes us from those who do not acknowledge the sovereignty of Christ in their lives. The Christian's standards are the standards of Christ and, in his entire conduct and disposition, he strives to reflect the image of Christ.

Christian discipleship implies an honorable way of life and the doing of good deeds. It is impossible to live in intimate harmony with Christ without something of His loveliness being reflected in our lives.

The litmus test of true Christlikeness is the love Christians have for one another. Good deeds without love lack the penetrating power of inspired discipleship, and faith then becomes a series of good deeds that lack meaning and purpose.

Christ fills us with the love that we lack so that we can achieve His purpose with our lives. If we find it difficult to love, we need only open our lives to His Spirit and allow Him to love others through us. As Christ's love flows through us, the world will see that we are His disciples.

YOUR CALLING TO BE CHRISTLIKE

"On that day you will realize that I am in My Father, and you are in Me, and I am in you." (John 14:20)

The life and teachings of Christ pose the greatest challenge that anyone can face. Many people who accept Him as their perfect example try to follow Him by committing themselves to doing good works. They make great sacrifices in the hope that this will help them to become like Him.

While all disciples should have a sincere desire to be like Jesus, all the effort and striving in the world will not help them to achieve this goal. Becoming like Christ begins in the heart and mind. This is where the presence of the living Christ is to be found; where He becomes the Source that enables them to grow spiritually in strength, beauty, and truth.

Unless the presence of Christ is a living reality in their hearts, they will not be able to reflect His personality in their lives.

The challenge and call to be more Christlike is intensely personal. It is a challenge to a deeper and more intimate relationship with the Master, in which you allow Him to reveal Himself through your life.

CHRISTLIKENESS

What we will be has not yet been made known.
But we know that when He appears,
we shall be like Him. (1 John 3:2)

The goal of every Christian should be to become like Jesus Christ. This will vary according to each person's nature and personality, but the desire will always be to grow into the likeness of the Master.

Unconditionally accepting the lordship of Christ is the beginning of a new and satisfying way of life. Because you belong to Him, your love and your mental and spiritual energy should be focused on becoming like Him.

Of course, trying to do this in your own strength will only lead to frustration and disappointment. Pray that He will give you His Holy Spirit. When you are united with Him, your faith comes alive and your whole life is lived in total obedience to Him.

Having a dynamic faith and obeying Christ will help you develop a Christlike character. Strangely, a person who has developed Christlike qualities because of his walk with the Lord, is often not aware of it. He has no hypocrisy or false pride and is too busy loving and serving God and others to have time to try and impress his fellow man.

WHAT IS A MATURE CHRISTIAN?

But grow in the grace and knowledge of our Lord and Savior Jesus Christ. (2 Peter 3:18)

Many people call themselves Christians because they were born in Christian homes or even because they are part of a Christian civilization. Nevertheless, they have never fully surrendered to Jesus.

True Christianity starts with the acceptance of Jesus Christ as your Savior and Redeemer. From that moment on you start living a new life. If this lifestyle is to be meaningful, you need to submit daily to the will of your Master.

Christ accepts you as His disciple and is true to all His promises, but the responsibility to develop a dynamic and living faith rests with you. You may have the desire to develop a richer prayer life, but unless you are willing to spend more time in prayer it will remain only a desire. You may long to have a stronger faith, but you must begin by using the faith you already have.

A committed and ripening Christian never stops cultivating his growth toward his goal of identifying with his role model, Jesus Christ. Christ is always with you to strengthen you in your weakness.

GOD IS WORKING THROUGH YOU

For it is God who works in you to will and to act according to His good purpose. (Philippians 2:13)

God has a plan for your life and within the framework of that plan you will find all you need to give full and perfect expression to the life God has given you.

You may be aware of your calling and destiny, yet not sufficiently to cause you to walk along the road God has laid out for you. You live your life arbitrarily and not according to God's will. This leads to frustration as you plod down blind alleys in your own strength, and are more conscious of your failures than your victories. Every door has to be forced open and few things seem to work out well for you.

When you realize that God is at work within you, and are determined to obey Him in all things, God becomes your partner in the art of living. Incredible things start to happen in your life. Obstacles either vanish, or you approach them with strength and wisdom from God. New prospects open in your life, extending your vision. You are filled with inspiration that unfolds more clearly as you move forward, holding God's hand.

MATURITY

Until we all reach unity in the faith and in the knowledge
of the Son of God and become mature, attaining to the
whole measure of the fullness of Christ. (Ephesians 4:13)

Intellectual and spiritual maturity do not occur as a
matter of course. It requires time and energy if you
wish to develop them to the fullness of the potential
within you.

In our efforts to reach maturity, we should have
a standard against which to measure our progress.
The apostle Paul teaches that this standard should
be nothing less than the character of Christ. It almost
sounds presumptuous to look at Christ and then
strive to reach His perfection and maturity in your
daily life. However, to aim any lower, is to accept a
second-rate Christianity.

When you compare what Christ is and what you
are, you could become pessimistic and decide that
this is not the life for you. However, never forget His
love for you and that He identifies with you in your
human frailty. He gives you the strength to lead a
godly life if you will only confess your dependence
on Him every moment of the day. Draw daily from
the strength that He puts at your disposal for this
very reason.

EXPERIENCE THE LIVING CHRIST

Since we live by the Spirit, let us keep in step with the Spirit. (Galatians 5:25)

Although there are divergent interpretations of the teachings of Christ, there is only one Christ and all things that are preached in His name must conform to Him. The living Christ can only be known through a personal relationship with Him, and by sharing in His love and power. This is achieved only through an intimate and personal relationship with Christ.

Your primary loyalty must be to the living Savior. How would He respond in situations in which you find yourself? What would He think of the under-handed business deal that you just clinched? How does He view relationships that are broken because of your unforgiving spirit?

The value of your faith and the depth of your spiritual experience can only be measured by their practical application in your daily life. You can spend hours at mass crusades; have the ability to pray in public; quote endlessly from the Word, but if you have not had a personal encounter with the living Christ your outward acts count for nothing.

BLUEPRINT FOR CHRISTLIKENESS

He has showed you, O man, what is good. And what does the LORD require of you? To act justly and to love mercy and to walk humbly with your God. (Micah 6:8)

In the midst of heated theological debates, the recurring question is, "What is a Christian?" Just knowing the Scriptures does not make someone a Christian. Many experts on the theory of Christianity are not Christians. In the same way, good deeds do not make one a Christian.

The core of our Christian faith is the acceptance of Jesus Christ as our Redeemer and Savior and our faith in Him. We need to open up our lives to Him so that His Holy Spirit can work in and through us to His honor and glory.

Jesus said, "Not everyone who says to me 'Lord, Lord' will enter the kingdom of heaven, but only he who does the will of My Father" (Matt. 7:21).

To do God's will means steadfastly obeying the commands of Christ. We must follow Him and love Him and serve our neighbor with love as long as we live. We must see to it that justice prevails by showing love and faith and living righteously before God. All this is possible in the strength of the Holy Spirit.

RENEW YOUR PERSONALITY

Therefore, if anyone is in Christ, he is a new creation; the old has gone, the new has come! (2 Corinthians 5:17)

Few people take the trouble to develop a pleasant personality. They may put on a fake smile and keep up a pleasant front for a special occasion but soon return to their old self.

Many people believe that personality cannot change, but this is not true. If it were, the sacrificial love of Christ would have been in vain. History shows us that sinners can become saints and that unlovable people can become pleasant when the love of Christ enters their hearts.

When you open yourself to the Spirit of the living Christ, your personality is transfigured and your lifestyle transformed. Your calling as a Christian is not merely to be a "good person" – although that is what you will become. Your first priority is to commit yourself completely to your Lord, and then your personality will be renewed. This will not happen through your own strength, abilities, and ingenuity, no matter how hard you try. When Christ gives you His Spirit, the impossible becomes possible. Our personality yields to Christ's influence and we grow into the likeness of our heavenly Example.

A WORTHY REPUTATION

They loved praise from men more than
praise from God. (John 12:43)

Your good reputation is priceless. It cannot be gained overnight, nor can it be bought by giving favors with hidden agendas. It can only be earned by living a noble life.

Standards that are founded on essential values ought not to be influenced by the opinions of other people. Your standards should not be of the world, but rather of God. If you allow your reputation to be shaped by other people's opinions and expectations of you, your life will be governed by ever-changing values. People have differing value systems, and you cannot comply with all of them.

When you live to please God alone, you develop a strong character and a good reputation according to His principles. Your word becomes your bond, your candor is tempered with love, honesty becomes an integral part of your being, and, because you are aware of your own vulnerability, you refrain from harshly criticizing others.

Living to please God has a powerful effect on your life. If you honor God and allow Him to govern your life, you will have the respect of those who honor God's standards.

CONFORMITY TO CHRIST

Jesus told him, "Go and do likewise." (Luke 10:37)

Bookshops have many shelves of books on the various aspects of Christianity. Hundreds of authors produce thousands of books that are read by millions of people who want to know more about Jesus. They try to expand their knowledge of the great scriptural truths.

While this is laudable, the danger exists that you could become so intrigued by your studies that you lose contact with the Christ about whom you are reading. You can know everything about Jesus, and yet not know Him personally.

Jesus taught the early disciples by His example, and that was the foundation of His church. This has not changed. People still respond to the Christian faith through the compassion and love they see in His modern-day disciples.

A thorough knowledge of the Scriptures is essential as a solid foundation for any believer, but never allow study to replace your personal relationship with Jesus. Neither should it hinder you from serving your fellow man as He served people when He walked this earth.

Tomorrow
MAY BE TOO LATE

Do not withhold good from those who deserve it,
when it is in your power to act. (Proverbs 3:27)

Sincere Christian compassion must be a spontaneous and true reflection of the love of Jesus Christ. He responded wherever He saw a need. He did not put people off or tell them to come back later. He did not take long to consider their requests or first discuss them with His disciples. Christ's entire life was a demonstration of His own words, "The Son of Man did not come to be served, but to serve, and to give His life as a ransom for many" (Matt. 20:28).

That is the example that we must follow if we want to live a life that conforms to Christ's. So often people hesitate when there is a need. Their unwillingness might be because of embarrassment or fear of becoming too involved in other people's affairs. They may be willing to offer temporary assistance, but the prospect of permanent involvement keeps them from offering help.

A person with a problem needs your help now; tomorrow other issues may arise that will make it too late. Jesus never hesitated to help others; dare you do differently?

HALF-HEARTED CHRISTIANITY

"I know your deeds, that you are neither cold nor hot. I wish you were either one or the other!" (Revelation 3:15)

Some people expect more from their faith than they deserve. They expect blessings without obeying God. They complain when they do not experience the presence of God, yet they neglect spending time quietly before God.

God gives His gifts of mercy and grace to those who are sincere in their commitment to Him. People who are willing to sacrifice time so that they can grow spiritually: who are disciplined in prayer and Bible study; who worship in spirit and truth.

Satisfactory Christianity can be experienced only when you have totally surrendered to God, and have cheerfully given Him everything you are and everything you have. Only such commitment will develop the glory, power, and beauty of Christ in your life.

It is tragic that so many Christians are satisfied with half-hearted commitment to Christ. They love Him, but are not willing to accept the challenges of that love. Placing Christ in the center of your life means complete surrender to Him. The reward is awesome.

DON'T MISS OUT ON THE BEST

But eagerly desire the greater gifts. (1 Corinthians 12:31)

It is natural to desire the best that life offers. However, it is of the utmost importance to know what is really best and not accept second best. Unfortunately this happens because people have a distorted understanding of values. They regard financial riches as of greater importance than an honorable character, that it is better to receive than to give, and that only a fool helps someone for nothing.

To know what is really the best for you, take stock of what you are and what you do. It takes courage to acknowledge your mistakes, understand your weaknesses, and be committed to doing something positive about your goals in life.

The highest standards are those given to man by God. They are the old, proven values of love, honesty, unselfishness, and purity. When you allow these God-given principles to govern your conscience, you will become aware of their challenge in your life, even though it may be difficult to adhere to them. But as you live according to these divine standards, God's best for you will outshine all the plans you can make for yourself.

LET OTHERS SEE CHRIST IN YOU

He said to them, "Go into all the world and preach the good news to all creation." (Mark 16:15)

Why do so many who call themselves Christians hesitate to confess their faith in Jesus before the world? Perhaps it is because of the ingrained expectations of society, which suggest that religion is taboo in polite company.

It is understandable that people are put off by those who are aggressively enthusiastic about their beliefs, but Christians need to be witnesses for Christ. We need to be unashamed of our faith in Jesus Christ. It is, however, important to know when to speak and when to be quiet.

There is one sure way to testify to your faith without offending other people, and that is to follow the example of Jesus. His whole life was a testimony of commitment to His duty, sympathy, mercy, and love for all people, regardless of their rank or circumstances. This is the very best way to be a witness for the gospel of Jesus Christ.

Ask the Holy Spirit to guide you so that others will see Christ in everything you do and say. In this way you will fulfill the command of the Lord.

TRUE SPIRITUALITY

"You are the light of the world. Let your light shine before men, that they may see your good deeds and praise your Father in heaven." (Matthew 5:14, 16)

For some, the word *spirituality* is not very popular. It conjures up images of well-meaning people who don't succeed in handling the practical problems of everyday life. Yet true spirituality is the most beautiful and powerful force known to humankind. It is able to handle all that life brings, because of the peace of mind that comes from continuous fellowship with the Lord.

The truly spiritual person is mainly practical. A truly spiritual employee will reveal his spirituality through excellent and honest work and service. A truly spiritual mother will reveal it through establishing a loving and well-organized family. Regardless of your role in life, you will fulfill it to the glory of God if you develop true spirituality.

The rich fruit of true spirituality is there for everyone to see. Fine sounding words and religious clichés can never be a substitute for true spirituality that loves Christ so much that His glory is reflected in holy lives. The essence of true spirituality is to love Christ with all your heart and mind and to allow His love to flow through you.

THE FRUIT OF THE SPIRIT

*But the fruit of the Spirit is love, joy, peace,
patience, kindness, goodness, faithfulness,
gentleness and self-control. (Galatians 5:22-23)*

Christian discipleship requires growth and the constant desire to become more and more like the Master in thought and deed. No serious follower of Christ can ignore the challenge to become more and more like Him.

The fruit of the Spirit are elements of the character of Christ. They have been called the nine main signs of God's presence, and can become part of the character of every disciple who commits himself to becoming like Christ. To enable you to achieve this, Christ promised Himself to you. That which is impossible for you becomes possible through Him.

Take one of the fruits and meditate on it during your quiet time until it becomes an integral part of your nature. Think about and affirm, "In Christ I am filled with love," until you feel His love fill your life. Do the same with all the other fruit over a period of time. This may sound like a time-consuming process, but spiritual growth cannot be hastened. In this way you will develop a well-balanced spiritual life, which you will live to His honor and glory.

SPARE A MOMENT FOR OTHERS

[Joseph] reassured them and spoke kindly to them. (Genesis 50:21)

In this merciless world, friendliness is a priceless quality. People are too busy with their own interests to even, for a moment, think about someone in distress.

The pressure and demands of business turn people into fiery and impatient tyrants. They constantly pursue better results and, in the process, drive their subordinates to the edge of despair. They might acquire much wealth, but they lose their peace of mind. They may have great power, but they lose the respect of the people with whom they work.

If you want a fulfilled life, start by caring about the feelings of others. Show interest in the welfare of your employer, fellow workers, and colleagues. Spare a moment to listen to their problems. Be tolerant and allow for their mistakes, because no man is perfect.

Follow the example of Christ, who showed sympathy and understanding toward all people. It will give you great satisfaction to know that you are supporting someone on the difficult path through life. There can be no greater reward than to know that you are continuing the work of the Master.

WHAT DO WE OWE?

Bear with each other and forgive whatever grievances
you may have ... Forgive as the Lord forgave you.
And over all these virtues put on love, which binds
them all together. (Colossians 3:13-14)

Courtesy is the outward expression of an inner spiritual maturity. If Christ lives in you, you will be kind and patient toward others.

Some people cultivate courtesy only to impress those who are easily deceived by appearances. A person who is truly courteous is humble and never tries to impress others. His attitude is the same regardless of whether he is talking to kings or beggars. He treats everyone alike, no matter what race, color, or creed they are. He rejoices in helping to make the path through life easier for others to travel.

It is impossible to say that you love and serve God while at the same time treating your neighbor with contempt and disrespect. Courtesy is not something that you can switch on and off. It is either an integral part of you, or an act of hypocrisy that is despised by your fellow human beings.

When the Holy Spirit lives in you, you reflect the qualities of Christ in your life. Love and courtesy are basic characteristics of the Christian life, and good manners are the product of true Christianity.

A MEANINGFUL LIFE

*A man's steps are directed by the LORD. How then can
anyone understand his own way? (Proverbs 20:24)*

When God controls your life, you learn to abide by
the guidelines of love, virtue, forgiveness, goodness,
faithfulness, compassion, and self-control. These are
God-given and God-inspired virtues.

In a truly spiritual life there is no room for pettiness or narrow-mindedness. To harbor a grievance
against someone, to refuse to forgive, to be thrilled
when someone else falls or fails are only a few symp-
toms of an immature spirit. And it is revealed in a
sickly, mean, and shallow attitude that is not part of
God's plan for your life.

If you sincerely strive to live according to God's
will, something of the greatness of your heavenly
Father will be revealed in your spirit as well as in your
attitude and actions. You will be able to distinguish
between what is important and what is unimportant.
You will develop a sensitivity that will enable you to
appreciate the small things in life, without allowing
them to divert your attention from the truly important
things. You will live to the glory of God and be guided
by His Holy Spirit. Under His protective hand, your
life will become meaningful.

ARE YOU A CHRISTIAN?

Follow my example, as I follow the example of Christ. (1 Corinthians 11:1)

How do you recognize a Christian? More to the point: how can others recognize Christ in you? If we try to answer these questions honestly and sincerely, they will invariably lead to earnest self-examination.

If you profess to being a Christian, it is your responsibility to manifest the characteristics of Christ in your life. No amount of biblical knowledge or church attendance can ever substitute for the reflection of the image of the Master in your life. However laudable good works may be, unless they are based on, and performed to, the honor and glory of Jesus Christ, they lose their impact and meaning.

Your entire life should reflect the sacrificial love, grace and forgiveness of Jesus. Then people will know that you are a true Christian. You should be tolerant and understanding.

Without being overly pious you should lead a life of integrity that in no way compromises your Christian standards. When you manifest Christlike qualities in your life, others will see that you truly love Christ.

LIVE LIKE
ROYAL CHILDREN

*For you did not receive a spirit that makes you a slave
again to fear, but you received the Spirit of sonship.
And by Him we cry, "Abba, Father." (Romans 8:15)*

There is a world of difference between confessing that you are a child of God and living like a child of God.

Many people profess their faith and yet live in constant fear. They suffer from a debilitating sense of inferiority and are unable to deal with life's problems. There is such a gap between what they should be and what they really are that they become despondent and abandon their faith.

When God made you His child, a new life began for you. Your sins were forgiven and you now stand in a new relationship to the King. Through His grace you belong to His kingdom. Because His Spirit now lives and works in you, your behavior towards people and your way of life have been revolutionized.

Your Father is the King of all kings. Knowing that He loves you and cares about you should give you inner peace. Steadfastly believing that He will guide you safely if you obey Him and love Him should be your comfort in life. Through Jesus Christ He invites you to call Him *Father*.

PIETY AND PRACTICE

So whether you eat or drink or whatever you do,
do it all for the glory of God. (1 Corinthians 10:31)

Many people think that being pious refers to a total inability to understand the basic issues of life and to live in an impractical fool's paradise. They are convinced that it is impossible to be godly and practical at the same time.

Unfortunately, many of God's children display a form of "holiness" that isolates them from the daily struggle, heartache, and pain of those for whom life is much harder. Jesus' holiness did not isolate Him from the pain and suffering around Him. On the contrary, He mingled with people and identified with their suffering and pain – that was why they were drawn to Him.

A godly life does not ignore the realities of life, assuming that all your problems will simply vanish. Christ needs agents of His love who wish only to do His will in the dynamic strength of His practical holiness.

If Christ lives in you (John 15:1-8) and you long for your life to reflect this, you will develop a practical piousness that will glorify God in the service of your fellow man.

TRUE HOLINESS

"For My thoughts are not your thoughts, neither are your ways My ways," declares the LORD. (Isaiah 55:8)

It is generally believed that living a holy life causes you to miss out on the "good things" of life. Many people find it incomprehensible that a life of fullness and joy is linked to holiness. Yet true holiness is the most dynamic, creative, and meaningful force in the world.

To be holy means having the right relationship with God. You enjoy life to the full and gain a greater understanding of people. True holiness consists of the burning desire to grow into Christlikeness and a willingness to identify with people. Thus the image of Christ is reflected in the community where you live.

Holiness urges one to live through the power of the Holy Spirit and results in a balanced approach to life. Nobody who strives to obtain holiness will ever find life monotonous or uninteresting, because they live in God's presence.

The secret of a balanced and gratifying life is to live in such a way that it is easy for the Master to express Himself through you. This is the way of true sanctification, and the road to a successful life.

A LIFE IN FULLNESS

For God did not call us to be impure, but to live a holy life. (1 Thessalonians 4:7)

It is extremely sad that many people think there is nothing as boring as living a "holy" life. Holiness has become synonymous with misery, and the average person longs for a pleasant life.

But "holiness" really means fullness of life – living well! God has called us to a full and fulfilling life. A truly spiritual life is balanced and practical. It has a pleasant maturity that causes others to trust. Holiness should be the goal of all spiritually-minded people, because it is the foundation of a mature life.

The path to holiness is as exciting and satisfying as the goal itself, because you travel this road with God, spending time in His divine presence. You cannot spend time with Christ and still remain the same person. Something of the character and personality of the eternal Father and Son penetrates your spirit and you become holy.

Blessed is the person whose feet are on the path of sanctification, because he experiences a fulfilled life.

IN PARTNERSHIP
WITH GOD

"Now let the fear of the LORD be upon you. Judge care-fully, for with the LORD our God there is no injustice or partiality or bribery." (2 Chronicles 19:7)

Some people believe that religion and business should be kept separate, while others become uncomfortable when they consider their business practices in the light of Christian principles.

God unequivocally has a place in your business practices and in your social life, just as He does in your spiritual life, and you cannot eliminate Him from one of these spheres without inflicting damage on yourself. Your entire life is governed by Christian principles and should testify of your Christianity, regardless of whether you are in a worship service or involved in activities outside of the church.

Integrity is one of the most important qualities in this respect. The surest way to reflect integrity in all your interactions is to make the living Christ your business partner. Whatever you do, scrutinize it through the eyes of Jesus; ask yourself how He would have reacted and what He would have done in your situation.

Follow Christ's example and you will be assured of a virtuous life that will earn you the respect of everyone who is part of your life.

DECEMBER

PRAISE AND THANKSGIVING

THE POWER OF PRAISE

My heart is steadfast, O God; I will sing and make music with all my soul. Awake, harp and lyre! I will awaken the dawn. (Psalm 108:1-2)

We often pray to thank God for what He has done for us, to lay our needs before Him, and to confess our sins to Him. It is sad but true, however, that we often neglect to express our praise of Him in prayer.

Never underestimate the power of praise in your life. If someone impresses you, you praise him to his face, or tell other people about him. Why shouldn't we then shower our benevolent God with praise? Think of all the remarkable things He has done, the miracles flowing from Him, the extraordinary extent of His love. Ponder for a moment the wonders of creation; of human life and achievement – and praise and glorify Him. He is indeed worthy of our love and thanksgiving.

If you focus on praising and glorifying God, you will create a very special relationship with the living Christ. Your prayer life will be transformed, and your love for Him intensified. Through your praise you will become a stronger witness for Him.

OUR WONDERFUL GOD!

*To our God and Father be glory for
ever and ever. (Philippians 4:20)*

The phrase, "praise the Lord," is repeated often in
the Psalms and the rest of the Bible. Some of God's
children continually praise and thank Him but
unfortunately many thousands take His goodness for
granted.

Some people anxiously beg God to help them in a
crisis. When God helps them, they don't give a second thought to the fact that the Almighty God, Creator of the universe, made man for His glory – and that
their gratitude will add to that glory.

It is worthwhile to pause and consider what your
life would have been like without the love and faithful care that God showers on you. How would you
have coped with insecurity and disappointment?
How would you have felt if there was nobody to love
or care for you?

Because you are a Christian, you don't have to worry about any of these things because your heavenly
Father knows exactly what you need. Give thanks to
the Lord, for He is good, His love endures for ever.

Praise and glorify God

Praise, O servants of the LORD, praise the name of the LORD. Let the name of the LORD be praised, both now and forevermore. (Psalm 113:1-2)

Why should God be praised and glorified? Why should we tell Him how almighty, all-knowing and loving He is? He commands us to praise Him. God never channels our energy into a dead-end. There is more to praising and glorifying God than simply repeating His divine attributes.

The complexity of the human temperament compels it to reach out to something higher and greater than itself. This yearning can be fulfilled by praising and glorifying God. It helps us connect to Him, who knows and understands the desires of our hearts. God does not need our praise, but we cannot cope without the strength and inspiration that emanate from our praise for Him.

True praise raises you up from spiritual despair and enables you to live in communion with your heavenly Father. Praise occurs in many different ways: during the excitement of a service; during the sanctity of communion; or in those quiet moments when you are alone with your heavenly Father. The method is of little importance, as long as it allows you to enter into the holy presence of God.

THE POWER OF THANKSGIVING

Heal me, O LORD, and I will be healed; save me and I will be saved, for You are the one I praise. (Jeremiah 17:14)

Psalm 47 appeals to all people to, "Clap your hands, all you nations; shout to God with cries of joy" (Ps. 47:1). It is impossible to clap your hands and sing exultantly to the glory of God and remain gloomy. Praise is a powerful stimulant. If you are feeling down-hearted and it seems as if nothing is working out well for you, then start praising and thanking God now.

True praise and thanksgiving to the almighty God should not depend on your feelings. It is precisely when you are feeling depressed, that you need to praise Him most.

Then you will experience the wonderful, uplifting power of praise and thanksgiving. It is the way in which you can overcome the negative influences that continually haunt you.

You don't need music or the church choir to truly praise and thank God. Simply lifting up your heart to Him brings you into His presence immediately and you cannot help but sing His praise and glory.

A GRATEFUL HEART'S BLESSING

*"He who sacrifices thank offerings
honors Me." (Psalm 50:23)*

The world is teeming with people who complain incessantly. Sometimes their complaints are valid but often they are born of a spirit of discontent. The danger of constant complaining is that it can become a habit. Eventually you forget that there are more things to be grateful for than to complain about. If you are presently complaining more often than expressing gratitude, you are living an inferior quality of life.

A grateful heart makes getting along with others easier and more rewarding; it deepens your understanding of life and makes those who live and work with you happier as well.

Never let a day go by without purposely expressing your gratitude. Open your eyes to the beauty around you and praise God for what you see or experience.

It is impossible to find someone who rejoices in God with constant praise and thanksgiving, but still suffers from depression at the same time. Human experience has proved over and over again that when you start thanking God for His gifts of grace, He is already planning the next blessing for you.

MAKE TODAY WONDERFUL

This is the day the LORD has made; let us rejoice and be glad in it. (Psalm 118:24)

Regardless of how bad things appear, God is greater than any situation you may find yourself in. You might doubt this truth, and, as a result, your life will be filled with fear and insecurity and each new day will be an almost unbearable burden.

Every new day is a unique gift to you from God. What you make of it is your responsibility. The way in which you welcome each day, will depend on your frame of mind and attitude toward life.

Fortunately, your frame of mind is not something that you have to leave in the hands of fate. You can mold it into a creative, constructive power. You were never meant to be the prey of changing emotions and fluctuating circumstances. God has given you the ability to choose your frame of mind as well as the pace of your life. Therefore you can live a happy, victorious life!

When you wake up in the morning, start the day on a positive note by praising God for His presence and His goodness. Then you will meet the day with joy and expectation.

YET I WILL REJOICE

Though the fig tree does not bud and there are no grapes on the vines, though the olive crop fails and the fields produce no food, ... yet I will rejoice in the LORD, I will be joyful in God my Savior. (Habakkuk 3:17-18)

It is easy to praise God when the sun shines. But when the threatening storm gathers and your prayers remain unanswered; when no one understands your problems, then it is easy to believe that God is no longer interested in you. Then praise seems to be impossible.

True praise is more than an emotional experience. It is figuratively looking into the face of God and sincerely asking, "Lord, what do You want me to do for You?" You may find the answer disconcerting. God may reveal to you truths about yourself that have long been hidden, truths like an unforgiving attitude, arrogance, bitter antagonism or some other sin that you refuse to discard.

When your life has been cleansed by the grace of God and the blood of Christ, you will experience a cheerfulness that will make it easy for you to praise God, even in misfortune and disaster. Then you will experience an indescribable joy that will call forth songs of praise from your heart.

GLORY BE TO GOD!

*Great is the L*ORD *and most worthy of praise;*
His greatness no one can fathom. (Psalm 145:3)

There are many reasons to glorify God. Not only did He create us and give us life, but He provides for our needs every day and places us in the community of the faithful, in whose midst we can grow to become the person whom He intended us to be. Above all, He reconciled us with Himself through Jesus Christ.

However, David has none of the above-mentioned in mind. Instead, he glorifies God simply because He is his great King. God's position alone makes Him worthy of all praise! Moreover, David not only glorifies the Lord, but bestows his blessing upon Him! What an overwhelming thought! A small measure of praise and blessing is bestowed upon God when we fellowship with Him in prayer and worship.

Reflect for a few moments on how God reigns over the great universe. Then glorify Him and bestow your blessing upon your great King of all kings!

A SONG OF PRAISE

Ascribe to the LORD, ascribe to the LORD ... glory and strength, ascribe to the LORD the glory due His name. Bring an offering ... worship the LORD in the splendor of His holiness. (1 Chronicles 16:28-29)

This song of praise was sung when the Ark of the Lord was brought back to Jerusalem after having been captured by the enemies of Israel. David called on the whole of creation to rejoice with him.

God deserves our unreserved praise, because He is the Creator of the whole earth. People like to honor champions and they delight in such rejoicing. God, as Conqueror, deserves our heartfelt songs of praise!

Plan to get out of the city this week and spend some time appreciating nature. See how creation rejoices in the works of God, and add your prayers of praise to the general chorus!

WITH A SONG IN YOUR HEART

Be filled with the Spirit. Speak to one another with psalms, hymns and spiritual songs. Sing and make music in your heart to the Lord. (Ephesians 5:18-19)

We are told to sing a new song to the glory of the Lord. A song expresses joy and love. The new song and gratefulness go hand in hand. A grateful person is a singing person and a singing person is a happy person, regardless of his circumstances.

Song and music are present everywhere in God's creation: the wind singing through the trees; the rhythmic sibilance of the waves; the sound of rain drops against the window; the whispering, waving wheat fields.

A new song proves that God rules in our hearts. The world can tell by our song that God lives in our hearts. There was a song when Christ was born – rejoicing songs of angels. Jesus sang a song of praise with His disciples on the night before His crucifixion. And in heaven the incessant song of the redeemed will resound forever.

Singing gives us courage in times of suffering. Like Paul and Silas, we should sing in the night of our suffering. May you encourage and strengthen other believers with your song.

APPRECIATE YOUR LIFE

*I will sacrifice a thank offering to You and call
on the name of the LORD. (Psalm 116:17)*

There are times when enthusiasm wanes and life
loses its sparkle. It suddenly seems that the positive
and meaningful life you once led is something of the
past.

To really appreciate life, retain your enthusiasm.
Do not take the gift of life for granted, or lose your
sense of anticipation and vision for the future. Enjoying and appreciating the beauty of life must be an
integral part of your life.

Do you appreciate the love and support of your
family? Can you still marvel at the rising of the sun?
Have you become so used to the suffering around
you that it no longer moves you with compassion?
Can you still laugh about a funny situation, or do you
find it hard to believe that humor is one of God's gifts
to you?

If you are appreciative, you can change your life
into a beautiful and exciting adventure. If you put God
at the center of your life and thoughts, you will discover that, by appreciating your life, you continually
move closer to Him, the Source of all real life.

COUNT YOUR BLESSINGS

"Whoever invokes a blessing in the land will do so by the God of truth." (Isaiah 65:16)

Many people go through life constantly moaning. If anyone praises a project or a person, they point out some fault. But the person who has developed the habit of counting his blessings, is extremely happy. He believes there is a solution for every problem and diligently looks for it. In the darkest moments he remains hopeful because he knows things will work out well.

To the optimist, the simple things in life are a constant source of joy – the gift of unrestrained laughter, the sympathy and understanding of loved ones, the bright rays of the sun.

The more you count your blessings, the more you will be aware of how many God pours into your life. Then your heart and mind will begin to overflow with gratitude for God's grace. When life becomes a burden and it feels as though you are living under an ominously dark cloud, counting your blessings is a sure way to restore your spiritual balance. Make a point of noticing God's abundant blessings in your life, appreciate them, and give Him thanks.

GRATITUDE

*Always giving thanks to God the Father for everything,
in the name of our Lord Jesus Christ. (Ephesians 5:20)*

Many Christians find life hard and demanding.
Wherever they turn they experience opposition and
discouragement. Nothing they attempt seems to work
out well.

Unfortunately many Christians have lost the art of
giving thanks. They are so overwhelmed by problems
that a cloud of depression has descended upon them,
and they can find very little to thank God for.

When a Christian stops giving thanks, he has lost
a source of great inspiration and spiritual strength.
First and foremost you should thank God for His love
and care. The thought of God's compassionate love
should fill your heart with sincere gratitude.

Thanksgiving is a powerful force in your spiritual
life. It can dispel the dark clouds of depression and
despair. The only way to release the power of thanksgiving is to practice it every day. Start each day with
a sincere prayer of appreciation to your heavenly
Father for the gift of life. You will discover that by
doing this, you will establish an atmosphere for the
day that will cause you to live in victory.

Rejoice in the Lord!

Then the people of Israel—the priests, the Levites and the rest of the exiles—celebrated the dedication of the house of God with joy. (Ezra 6:16)

Unfortunately, many people attend church services as little more than a duty done merely for habit's sake. The tragedy of an attitude like this is that it deprives people of the greatest of all joys: joy in the Lord.

God invites you to receive abundant life. If you turn to Him you will become increasingly aware of His life-giving Spirit working in you. Seemingly unattainable goals will suddenly be within your reach. Setbacks no longer overwhelm you because in Him you find the strength to overcome. A newly found confidence replaces your nervous anxiety and sense of failure. Day by day your faith grows stronger.

As you open yourself to the Spirit, your worship, Bible study, and prayer life gain new meaning. If you place your trust in the living Christ, you will discover that God is no longer a far-away figure, but an integral part of your life.

Worship ought to be a joyful experience. Open yourself to the Holy Spirit, and He will raise you from despondency to ecstasy in Christ.

INEXHAUSTIBLE POWER

*But those who hope in the LORD will renew their strength.
They will soar on wings like eagles; they will run and not
grow weary, they will walk and not be faint. (Isaiah 40:31)*

Some religious aspects become clichés and lose their deeper meaning. Spiritual disciplines that once fortified your faith may have become an obstacle that prevent you from growing spiritually. You may have addressed God as *Father* for so long that you have come to think of Him as a gray old lord who closes His eyes to your sins, thus forgetting that He is also a God who punishes sin.

To regard God with respect and awe moves you to true worship. You cannot spend time contemplating the wonder of God and His truths revealed through Christ, and remain spiritually weak and ineffectual. There is power in praising and worshiping Him.

Develop an attitude toward life that is constantly on the lookout for opportunities to praise and thank God. Let the thought of praising Him dominate your thoughts, and you will feel the power of the almighty God flowing through your life.

BE CONTINUALLY GRATEFUL

Continue to live in Him, rooted and built up in Him, strengthened in the faith as you were taught, and overflowing with thankfulness. (Colossians 2:6-7)

It is easy to be unhappy and ungrateful when so many people restlessly pursue empty utopian dreams of a better life. Discontent creates a negative outlook on life, and a restricted and purposeless lifestyle that finds fault with everything. People focus so much on the flaws and faults around them that they fail to see the wonders of God and His grace.

Every detail of your life is known to God. Although things sometimes go wrong, God is not to blame. However, He can change your situation so that light radiates out of the darkness and hope is born from despair.

If you feel dejected, think back on all the good things that have happened in your life. Recall those times when you were overwhelmed by Christ's presence and His love filled your entire being. Thank the Lord for His grace and blessings. Then the Holy Spirit will start His healing work in you and you will once again see life in a positive light. Praise and gratitude lift the heart and honor God who gives good gifts to men.

THE BLESSING OF GRATITUDE

And whatever you do, whether in word or deed, do it all in the name of the Lord Jesus, giving thanks to God the Father through Him. (Colossians 3:17)

In the hustle and bustle of everyday life, it is easy to forget about ordinary courtesy. People do nice things for us, shop assistants serve us with courtesy and a smile. But we forget that a word of appreciation could change their routine into a blessing.

The habit of saying *Thank you* enriches every aspect of our lives. Always be ready to express thanks. You will soon discover how much joy you can bring to others. Apart from the fact that you enrich and bless the lives of others, your own life will be enriched. Never underestimate the power of gratitude.

If this is true on an ordinary human level, how much more will our lives be enriched if we learn to express gratitude toward our Heavenly Father. All that we have, He gave to us, and yet we so seldom thank Him. When we do, our spirit is set free and we experience a joy and blessing that only God can give. When you thank God for His immeasurable love and all His blessings, you will experience true festive joy.

THE SECRET OF A FESTIVE LIFE

Be joyful always; pray continually; give thanks in all circumstances, for this is God's will for you in Christ Jesus. (1 Thessalonians 5:16-18)

In every life, something special and divine is hidden. If Christ abides in you through faith, you develop a keener appreciation of the beauty and depth that are hidden in the lives of your fellow men, and in the world around you. If you live in the Spirit of Jesus Christ, you will develop a greater appreciation of life; and the greater your appreciation, the more life will reveal its hidden treasures to you.

The example of the ten lepers, of whom only one came back to thank Jesus, shows us that Jesus appreciates gratitude.

The Scriptures resound with a triumphant note of gratitude as people expressed their appreciation to God for all His blessings. God is our Father and we love Him for His own sake and not for His blessings. He is infinitely patient and His dealings with us are so merciful. How can we withhold our appreciation for all the good things He gives us?

You draw near to God when you praise and glorify Him, showing your appreciation. He becomes very real to you and your life becomes a continual feast.

A GIFT FOR THE CHILD

Then they opened their treasures and presented Him with gifts of gold and of incense and of myrrh. (Matthew 2:11)

It is hard to understand that God, the Giver of every good and perfect gift, finds pleasure in receiving gifts from those who love Him. Of course, everything we own belongs to Him, but we can give back to Him the treasures He gives us to care for.

There is one thing the Master finds more precious than anything else: the love of your heart. Whatever we offer Him, whether treasures, time, or service, has little value unless it is sanctified through our love for Him.

This gift makes all people equal in the eyes of God. There are those who can bring Him pure gold, fragrant frankincense, or precious myrrh; others can only bring Him a coin; and others don't even have that to give Him. But the Lord looks beyond the gift to the love that motivates the giver.

How can we bring these love-inspired gifts to Jesus? Find someone in need. Then offer your help in the Name of the great, merciful One. Become a friend to the lonely, comfort those who are sorrowful, feed the hungry. Above all, in gratitude, give yourself to Him completely.

IMMANUEL
– GOD WITH US!

*The Word became flesh and made His dwelling
among us. We have seen His glory, the glory of
the One and Only, who came from the Father,
full of grace and truth. (John 1:14)*

Many people in Bethlehem were not even aware that
Jesus had been born in a stable. The possibility that He
could be the long-awaited Messiah did not even cross
their minds. Those who did expect the Messiah, were
looking for someone radically different, the "Wonderful Counselor, Mighty God, Everlasting Father,
Prince of Peace" (Isa. 9:6).

It was unthinkable that He would come to them
in such utter poverty, without all the pomp and cer-
emony that usually accompanied a royal birth. Yet
this was indeed the Child who had come to change
the history of the world.

Nations and empires have prospered and waned,
but this Child still has an immeasurable influence on
all humanity. He still inspires the humble at heart to
great heights and still changes cowards into heroes.

May He protect you and may He bless and keep
you and your loved ones. May you experience the
presence of the risen, living Christ every day of this
Christmas season and may this fill your heart with
great joy.

IF CHRIST HAD NOT COME

"If I had not come and spoken to them, they would
not be guilty of sin. Now, however, they have
no excuse for their sin." (John 15:22)

It is rather poignant when Christ Himself says, "If I had not come ... "

We would have found ourselves in a world without the joy of Christmas: no Christmas cards, no presents, no family get-togethers, and no Christmas blessings. Yet, the danger is that we can celebrate Christmas but forget about Christ because we relegate Him to the outskirts of our celebrations.

If Christ had not come we would have lived in a world without the message of love. The good news of Christmas is that God loves us, we love God, and we love one another – and this is possible only because Jesus came!

If Christ had not come we would have lived in a world without the gospel. There would have been no salvation, no baptism, no holy communion. We would have had to carry the burden of our own sin because there would have been no cross of reconciliation for us.

If Christ had not come we would have no hope for the future. But, praise the Lord! Christ has come! Hallelujah!

YOUR SALVATION IS HERE!

The LORD has made proclamation to the ends of the earth: "Say to the Daughter of Zion, 'See, your Savior comes!'" (Isaiah 62:11)

At Christmas we commemorate the coming of Christ into the world, but we must never forget about the coming of Christ into our hearts. His advent in the flesh as the Lamb of God that takes away the sins of the world, glorious as it is, means nothing unless we personally partake of His salvation.

If we want to experience the real joy of Christmas, Christ has to inhabit our hearts with His salvation and peace. Thank God that Christ not only came into the world, but personally comes into the hearts of those who believe in Him.

He came to find and redeem those who were lost, and He gave everyone who accepted Him the right to become a child of God (see John 1:12). Do you believe this? Do you believe that He comes to where you are, anxious and overwhelmed by your own sin?

He comes to you with His hands filled with grace and forgiveness and blessings; He comes to turn your sadness into joy. Christmas is essentially a feast of salvation, because your Savior came!

THE CORE TRUTH OF CHRISTMAS

*This is how God showed His love among us: He sent
His one and only Son into the world that we
might live through Him. (1 John 4:9)*

The most astonishing truth about Christmas is that
God loves us. God is love and He loves us with a love
that gives only the best and most valuable, as with
Christmas when He gave us His Son. He also loves us
with a love that forgives and cares.

Since God so loved us, we also ought to love one
another, says the apostle John (see 1 John 4:11). Love
must triumph in our everyday lives: in our marriages,
in our home lives, and in all our relationships – in
word and deed.

Christ grew up to become a Man of sorrow at
Golgotha and in Gethsemane. Therefore we, as His
followers, also do not remain infants in faith or restricted by a faith that never goes beyond the stable
where our Savior was born. We must grow to spiritual
maturity.

Like the shepherds, we must also be loving witnesses and praise God for everything we have heard
and seen. We must proclaim the wonder of His love:
redemption, grace, and peace.

GLORY TO GOD IN THE HIGHEST!

Suddenly a great company of the heavenly host appeared with the angel, praising God and saying, "Glory to God in the highest, and on earth peace to men on whom His favor rests." (Luke 2:13-14)

For the average person, life was not noticeably different on the night of Jesus' birth. Bars and taverns were busy serving clients. Shepherds crouched around their fires to keep warm while they kept watch over their sheep.

But in an isolated corner of Bethlehem, in the stable of a modest inn, a Baby lay in a manger. And when the shepherds were preparing for sleep, the angels gathered in a mighty choir and the silence of the night was broken by celestial hymns of praise. Imagine the shepherds reaction: shock, fear, and awe. They knew that they had to find this extraordinary Child whose birth the angels had announced.

While commemorating and celebrating the joyous birth of Christ on this day, make sure that you personally seek Jesus and find Him, as the shepherds did on that very first Christmas night so many years ago. Use the angels' song as your prayer to rejoice in the birth of your Savior.

CHRIST IS BORN!

*Jesus was born in Bethlehem in Judea,
during the time of King Herod. (Matthew 2:1)*

It is an irrefutable historical fact that Jesus was born in Bethlehem. Through His physical birth, God revealed Himself to all of humanity.

He who was born in Bethlehem more than two thousand years ago is still being born in the hearts and lives of people today. This simple but overwhelming truth is often lost in the chaos of our busy lives.

In spite of the festivities around Christmas time, if you have not experienced the birth of Christ in your personal life, you will never know the true joy and peace of Christmas. Only Christ gives depth and peace to the joy of Christmas. The birth of Christ in Bethlehem is a mere historical fact and nothing more than that, until He is born in your life. Then you not only know Christmas, but you also know the Christ of Christmas.

If you want to experience true Christmas joy, Christ must be born in your life and you must place Him in the center of your entire life. When His holiness permeates your life, it becomes "a merry Christmas" in the true sense of the word.

PRAISE AND THANK GOD

The shepherds returned, glorifying and praising God for all the things they had heard and seen. (Luke 2:20)

The festivities are over: the wilted Christmas tree has been thrown out; the glossy paper is crumpled; party hats lie torn and tattered in a corner; the decorations and balloons flap pitifully in the breeze. The excitement and joy that people associate with Christmas is now something of the past and everybody returns to the everyday routine of life.

But this should not be the case! The joyous event that we celebrate on Christ's birthday does not end there. This event reminds us of the unfathomable love of God for His children for all eternity. The Christ Child in the stable of Bethlehem is the Savior of the world. Through His Holy Spirit He offers you true life. He wants to guide you in love on His path of righteousness every hour of the day.

Certainly, Christmas is a day of exuberant celebrations when we attempt to thank God for the gift of His Son. And yet, today and every day should be reason enough for you to praise and thank God for the presence of the living Christ who is with you, every day of your life.

JOYOUS CHRISTIANITY

"My soul glorifies the Lord and my spirit rejoices in God my Savior." (Luke 1:46-47)

Many people view their faith as a heavy and unbearable burden. They frown upon any semblance of light-heartedness in spiritual matters. They stoop somberly under the heavy burden of their spiritual conscience.

But the faith of the Christian should be a joyous experience. Your Father takes joy in and is interested in your life. He is happy when you are happy; He consoles you in sadness and grief; He supports you when the burden becomes too much for you; He helps you up when you stumble over obstacles and He enjoys your successes as you enjoy them yourself.

Christianity does not eliminate joy and happiness from life. Through your communion with the living Christ, you live in the blessing of His presence every day. The more you praise and thank Him, the more happiness you glean from your spiritual life.

Your surrender and devotion should be such that the joy of the Lord radiates across the entire spectrum of your life. Then every day becomes a joyous celebration of Christ.

MEDITATION

*When anxiety was great within me, Your consolation
brought joy to my soul. (Psalm 94:19)*

We are left with the burnt-out ashes of the old year,
while the new year is only a dim glimmer ahead of
us. As the year dies, we are tempted to look back.
Unfortunately, many people dwell on failures, disappointments, and other misfortunes, causing anxiety
for the year ahead.

To meditate on the past has its rightful place in
your life, but it should always be done constructively.
Learn from past mistakes without being weighed
down by their burden. At the same time, be careful
not to rest on your laurels, congratulating yourself
on the successes achieved during the past year. These
should only serve as an inspiration for you to strive
for more and to work even harder in the year that lies
ahead.

Determine to enter the new year in the company
of Christ, under the guidance of the Holy Spirit. Let
Christ be your example and your guide. Let your
mind become sensitive to the voice of the Holy Spirit,
and choose to follow His will under all circumstances.
Then you will experience God's peace and consolation that will bring joy to your soul.

ALL'S WELL
THAT ENDS WELL

Give thanks to the Lord, for He is good;
His love endures forever. (Psalm 106:1)

I know to Whom I have entrusted myself,
even when my light turns to darkness.
I know the Rock on Whom I have built,
He is the One Who is my salvation.

With these words we leave the old year behind and enter into the new year. Now, in the last moments of this year, we can see the complete journey God mapped out for us this past year. We praise Him for every step of our pilgrimage, because He loved us all the way.

We have to beg forgiveness for many things: precious hours that we wasted, love we withheld, prayers we never prayed, opportunities we neglected. There are also innumerable reasons why we can thank our Lord: for protection; for healing; for support; for our daily bread.

May we find inspiration in the words of Marie Louise Haskins, "Put your weak hand in the mighty hand of God, then step out into the dark with courage. It will be far better for you than a light, and safer than a familiar road."

GOD'S PERFECT METHOD

"He has done everything well." (Mark 7:37)

Christians like to conclude the year that has come to an end in the presence of God, and enter the new, unknown year under the guidance of His merciful and loving hand.

With the Word in our hand, we look back on the road we have traveled, and ask that He illuminate the road stretching ahead with His friendly light. What we have learned from the year that has past is much more important than the chronological time it filled.

God has done so much in our lives, filling it with purpose and significance because of His undeserved grace. We can merely say, "Everything He does is good." Not everything we experienced was joyous, but that is not necessarily bad. Sometimes God tests us with grief, but this, too, is for our own good.

When we reach the end of life's pilgrimage, as we have reached the end of this year, we will clasp our hands in amazement and humbly confess that He did all things well. Knowing this, we can bid farewell to the old year with peace of mind.

Peace until the end

"I am the Alpha and the Omega," says the Lord God,
"who is, and who was, and who is to come,
the Almighty." (Revelation 1:8)

And so we reach the last day of the old year. There are many things we are ashamed of, but many that we are thankful for. There are regrets for missed opportunities, but we have received so much grace from God. The year brought grief, but also joy; defeat, but also victory; storms, but also sunshine.

God is still our Father, a privilege beyond compare. Let us, therefore, count our blessings today, knowing that He remains constant – yesterday, today, and forever.

You are richer today than you were yesterday if you smiled often; gave something of yourself to others; forgave your enemies; made new friends; turned problems into opportunities. You are richer today than you were yesterday if you noticed God's handiwork; if you learned what is really important in life; if you have a little more patience with others' faults.

You are rich today if a child smiled at you; a dog licked your hand; if you looked for the best in others, and if you gave the best of yourself to others and to God. Then you enter the new year secu

PEACE UNTIL THE END

"I am the Alpha and the Omega," says the Lord God,
"who is, and who was, and who is to come,
the Almighty." (Revelation 1:8)

And so we reach the last day of the old year. There are many things we are ashamed of, but many that we are thankful for. There are regrets for missed opportunities, but we have received so much grace from God. The year brought grief, but also joy; defeat, but also victory; storms, but also sunshine.

God is still our Father, a privilege beyond compare. Let us, therefore, count our blessings today, knowing that He remains constant – yesterday, today, and forever.

You are richer today than you were yesterday if you smiled often; gave something of yourself to others; forgave your enemies; made new friends; turned problems into opportunities. You are richer today than you were yesterday if you noticed God's handiwork; if you learned what is really important in life; if you have a little more patience with others' faults.

You are rich today if a child smiled at you; a dog licked your hand; if you looked for the best in others, and if you gave the best of yourself to others and to God. Then you enter the new year secu